Wall Street on $20 a Month

How to Profit from an Investment Club

Phyllis A. Humphrey

A Wiley Press Book
John Wiley & Sons, Inc.
New York   Chichester   Brisbane   Toronto   Singapore

Library of Congress Cataloging-in-Publication Data

Humphrey, Phyllis A.
  Wall Street on $20 a month.

  Bibliography: p.
  1. Stocks — United States.   2. Speculation.
3. Investments — United States.   I. Title.   II. Title:
Wall Street on Twenty dollars a month.
HG6049.H86   1986   332.63'22   85-22503
ISBN 0-471-84038-6

Printed in the United States of America
86 87 10 9 8 7 6 5 4 3 2 1

Model Portfolio on page 75 courtesy Kenneth Janke, *Better Investing* Magazine, © 1985 National Association of Investors Corporation.

Sample page from the Value Line Investment Survey on page 77 courtesy Value Line, Inc., © 1985.

Side one of the Standard & Poor's report on page 78 courtesy Standard & Poor's Corp., © 1985.

The N.A.I.C. Stock Selection Guide on pages 81 and 82 courtesy the National Association of Investors Corporation, © 1983.

Computer program printouts on pages 103 and 104 courtesy Criterion House, Foster City, CA 94404.

The N.A.I.C. Stock Comparison Guide on page 116 courtesy the National Association of Investors Corporation, © 1974.

The N.A.I.C. Portfolio Management Guide on page 117 courtesy the National Association of Investors Corporation, © 1980.

Page 124, Chart by Securities Research Company, A Division of United Business Service Co., 208 Newbury St., Boston MA 02116.

Daily Price Graph on page 131 courtesy Leonard Raiser, *Better Investing* Magazine, © 1984 National Association of Investors Corporation.

Symphony and "123" are trademarks of Lotus Development Corp.

"Hercules Graphics Card" is a trademark of Hercules Computer Technology.

Readers should refer to the Investors Manual published by the National Association of Investors, 1515 East Eleven Mile Road, Royal Oak, MI 48067, for a full explanation of the use of the NAIC Stock Selection Guide.

To my husband, Curt,
for his loving and unfailing support

Contents

Foreword

The way most people end up with a million dollars in the stock market is to start out with two million dollars. That's right! Most folks lose money investing in stocks. They do so because they make a number of common mistakes. Mostly they do so because they haven't a consistent and sound investment program to stick to which offers potential investment success. Successful investors must know what to do, and then stick to it. The others don't know what to do, and even if they did, their emotions sometimes get in the way of sticking to it. The market has its own perverse way of creating investors who end up complaining, "I knew better than to do that."

It needn't be like that for you. If you're one of the lucky Americans who is extremely wealthy you may be able to hire some top-flight investment manager to handle your money for you. There are a number, but not a large number, who have done consistently well over the years. Be sure to check a long list of client references up one side and down the other before retaining an investment manager or advisor.

If you aren't that wealthy, or just plain want to do it yourself, an outstanding way to get started on Wall Street is outlined by Phyllis Humphrey. As she shows, anyone can make a good return through an investment club, or as an individual investor, by paying attention to some simple rules. You can learn a lot and have fun along the way. And the best part is that it doesn't cost an arm and a leg. You needn't put up your life savings. Only $20 a month will get you on your way.

In my ramblings through a lot of radio call-in talk shows, it has consistently amazed me how few individuals know how to navigate the investment currents. Participation in an investment club will give you a world of education and a form of self-discipline to keep you on the right track.

Phyllis Humphrey is perhaps the ideal pathfinder to show us the way to successful low-cost investing. She has no fancy degree from Stanford's Graduate School of Business. She didn't start under the training of a leading investment guru. A wife and mother and former public relations director of a local shopping center, she started an investment club, and bango—she generated better returns over many years than most professionals do. She had her picture on the cover of a national magazine and had her club featured in *Money* magazine, not to mention numerous local papers, and wrote investment articles for magazines ranging from *Fact* to *Savvy*.

If you've been getting great returns in the stock market for years, you may not need this book. But if you've lost money and never known why, or you're just beginning to consider investing, I can't think of a better way to get started right, without spending much money, than via a solid grounding and one of the programs outlined in Phyllis's book, *Wall Street on $20 a Month*.

KENNETH L. FISHER

Mr. Fisher is founder and Chief Executive of Fisher Investments, Burlingame, California, a *Forbes* magazine columnist, and author of the Dow Jones–Irwin best-seller, *Super Stocks*.

Preface

Eighteen years ago, when I began to read about the stock market, there were few books that told the "small investor" how to make money in Wall Street. And virtually all of those classified the small investor as someone with "only" $10,000, at a time when that amount would buy a house in some parts of the United States!

But I've discovered that you don't need $10,000 to start, or even $1,000. One man, investing $20 a month in a program similar to the ones in this book, saw his total investment of a mere $6,000 become a nest egg of $23,000 in twenty-five years. Another, putting only $10 a month in an investment club since 1941 (a total of $4,800) is now worth $95,000!

This book won't tell you how to become a millionaire overnight. What it will tell you is how thousands of people have turned $20 a month, (or $10 or $25) into a nice chunk of money to make a down payment on a house, help put children through college, finance a small business, or put extra cash aside for emergencies or retirement.

Best of all, there is no "one" way to do it; three ways are described in this book, together with complete details for getting you started in the right direction.

In my opinion, the best way, and the way I turned $2,000 into more than $6,000 in about nine years, is to start or join an investment club; and you'll find surprisingly simple instructions for doing it that way in chapters 4–6. However, if you prefer not to try an investment club, there are still two more ways to invest small sums, described in chapters 7–13 — and they're *not* mutual funds!

PHYLLIS A. HUMPHREY

Whichever way you prefer at the moment, please read the entire book, as most of the information in each chapter is relevant to other chapters.

As you'll learn in the following pages, I'm extremely enthusiastic about investment clubs, but more than that, I'm enthusiastic about investing in the stock market, and I think it's not just for the wealthy anymore. The "little guy" (or "gal") can make money there too.

Acknowledgments

I want to take this opportunity to thank all the members, past and present, of my investment club, and the following persons who have been of special help: Carole Di Camillo, Kenneth Hrubes, Dorothy Smirle, Kenneth Fisher, Mary Zimmerman, June Lee, Paula Payne, Charlie Keith, Barbara Gallagher, Al Alward, Larry Tissot, and Dr. Paul Brose. Special thanks to my agent Helen McGrath, and Tom O'Hara and Kenneth Janke of N.A.I.C.

Why Wall Street?

My fascination with the stock market began in my teenage years, even though my parents owned no shares of stock; nor did anyone else in my family. We were "poor," and trading in the stock market seemed reserved for the affluent.

Although they shared my economic as well as my physical neighborhood, many of my young friends hoped for wealth one day. Some trusted that superior athletic ability or business acumen or discovering oil or inventing a better gadget would bring them success, fame and fortune, and everything that money could buy: jewels, furs, mansions with servants, and trips abroad. Many of them, in spite of penniless backgrounds, dreamed that somewhere lived a prosperous relative who would die and leave everything to them.

My dreams, however, revolved around that magic place called Wall Street, where fortunes were made overnight, at least in the books I read. That those fortunes sometimes disappeared just as quickly never fazed me; I hoped to be one of the lucky ones.

My chance finally came while I was working as a secretary in a manufacturing company that merged into another firm. Offered the opportunity to buy the newly issued stock, I purchased ten shares at $10 each—a lot of money for me at that time—and a year later, needing a down payment to buy a car, I sold them for $240 less commissions. No wonder making money in the stock market looked easy.

An appreciation of 140 percent in one year never occurred again, but my investing has done rather well lately, sandwiched in between keeping a home, raising children, running a small business, free-lance writing, and enjoying a few hobbies. The investment club I started with thirteen others in 1972 earned 175 percent in its first nine years. That averaged out, with each of us depositing only $20 a month, to 18.57 percent on a true annual basis, a very high return for that period.

Since many people have asked how I did it, I've put down the way it worked for me, confident that my achievement can be duplicated by anyone with a few dollars that won't be missed, a few hours of study per month, and some common sense.

First, you should have some form of insurance and some money in a safe or insured medium to take care of emergencies. That's only sensible. Although I advocate ownership of common stocks and strongly believe that only in the rarest of circumstances do you incur the risk of losing it all in the market, I do think investing should be in the third place on your list for your extra money.

Second, I assume you know something about the stock market and how it operates. If not, perhaps all your questions will be answered in Chapter 3 or in the Glossary at the end of this book.

This is a book about investing in the stock market, not about other forms of investments. It's not about banks, savings and loans, thrift institutions, Treasury bills, money market funds, or insurance. Nor is it about coins, stamps, art, antiques, other collectibles, real estate, or tax shelters.

Even within the field of equities, this book is not about related investments, such as mutual funds, bonds, commodities, options, or even about preferred or convertible stocks.

So many various avenues for investing one's money exist, whether for earning interest or for capital appreciation, that it would (and does) take a great deal of study and application to be familiar with even a smattering of the myriad choices and their many intricacies. The necessity to keep up with what happens to them, in the rapidly changing world of the eighties, takes more time than the average person can spare from daily activities.

All investment areas may be worthy of attention by someone at some time, but they're not within the scope of this work, which will deal exclusively with direct purchase and sale of common stocks.

Even within this narrow range, it is impossible to know all one might wish to know about investing. To begin with, there are over 2,000 companies traded daily on the New York Stock Exchange alone and almost 800 on the American Stock Exchange; including those traded in regional exchanges and over the counter, there are some 40,000 publicly owned companies in the United States. To become familiar with even a thousandth of these possibilities for investing in common stock is clearly no simple task.

In addition, you'll want some knowledge of how the stock market works, what the forces behind price movements are, how to evaluate companies (fundamental analysis), as well as what factors are inherent in the market itself (technical analysis).

I'm narrowing the choices so drastically not only to reduce the amount of time spent in understanding the areas of investment, but also because I believe that investment in common stock is one of the easiest, safest, and most enjoyable ways to provide for the future, stay ahead of inflation, and work toward the continuance of the free enterprise system, which enabled this country to become the richest and most respected nation in the world in its first 200 years of existence.

IT'S EASY

I won't pretend that there is a magic formula and once you know it, you'll be on the road to riches for the rest of your life. Reading and studying must be done; even then, there's no guarantee you'll even increase your capital, much less see it grow at a superior rate. All I can tell you is that it has been done, and is being done, by thousands of ordinary people.

Moreover, it's less difficult to learn common stock investing than to become an expert in most other avenues of investment, such as real estate, coins, collectibles, etc.

"Easy" is a relative term. Investing in common stocks is more difficult than putting your money in a bank savings account and merely letting it earn interest, but taking the easy road may mean not keeping up with inflation. Since 1939, the dollar has shrunk to thirteen cents. Between 1962 and 1984, consumer prices rose 5.7 percent, but the yearly return on stocks averaged 8.8 percent. In fact, the stock market has always outpaced inflation. Going all the way back to 1878, you'll find consumer prices rose 2.2 percent annually, but stocks returned 8.5 percent.

Many books have been written about how to make millions in real estate. I'm not disparaging them. I think everyone should own a home if he or she wishes and can afford it. Certain types of real estate investment can provide both income and tax shelter. And there's no doubt that many people indeed made their fortunes that way. But easy it's not. Not every person who bought real estate as an investment turned ten thousand dollars into a million in ten easy years.

I know people who bought property in the wrong section of town and watched it deteriorate and drop in value. Some unhappy landlords saw their rental units destroyed by vandalism, unrented for months while the mortgage payments continued, or occupied by deadbeats who couldn't legally be removed for several months (with no rent paid). Many landlords spent all their spare time fixing up their units, repairing appliances, and worrying about vacancies.

Before buying property, they spent months visiting neighborhoods, looking at vacant land, houses, apartments, condominiums. In addition, they had to learn about principal, interest, taxes, insurance, closing costs, escrow, financing through conventional mortgages, the FHA, veterans' loans, or "creative financing" brought on by tight money, and a host of things that, since I am not involved in real estate, I probably can't even think of. Compared to that, investing in the stock market seems easy to me.

Yes, you can make money in real estate. At any rate, you could have in the past thirty years. Whether it's still possible is a question that even the experts can't answer. Inflation has skyrocketed the price of houses, from an average of $10,000 just after World War II, to more than $100,000 today.

Property taxes, also rising dramatically, threatened disaster to those on fixed incomes, so that in 1976 California residents rose up and passed legislation (the famous Proposition 13) to curtail what they considered excessive taxation. Since then other states have enacted similar laws; but legislators are busy finding loopholes in them and looking for ways around them.

In the early eighties interest rates reached their highest level in the history of the nation, forcing many would-be home owners out of the market entirely and making real estate investment a long-term negative-cash-flow proposition.

Although the current rate of inflation has dropped, interest rates remain in the double-digit range. Depending on the sentiments that prevail in Washington, D.C., over the next few years, and whether Congress finally does something about the budget deficit, the interest rates may finally drop or they may return to astronomical levels. Inflation, too, may escalate again.

At this writing, the federal government is considering several versions of a "flat" income tax rate. If the one called "Treasury II" is passed, the result will be loss of property tax deductions and loss of interest cost deductions on all but a personal residence, or, to put it another way, the loss of two of the prime benefits (in some cases the only ones) of real estate investment.

It's not beyond the realm of possibility that we may see another recession in the next few years, or even a depression. This is a risky world for someone with limited amounts of money to invest.

If studying real estate is difficult, consider trying to learn about coins and stamps, antiques, or art and collectibles. Once again, your time is no longer your own; you must study, perhaps attend stamp auctions or antique shows and compete with experts. Wrong judgments can cost you dearly.

While it's true you may enjoy your investments — especially in the case of art or antiques — by having them in your home to look at, there's always the risk of theft or vandalism, and your insurance rates will escalate. There's also a limit to how many of them you can keep in your home; any excess must be stored elsewhere with attendant storage costs. Yes, if you enjoy art and antiques, by all means buy them. But they're very risky as investments for the future, especially if you don't know what you're doing.

Investing in common stocks, on the other hand, can be easier because there is so much help for you along the way. Besides books you can find in the libraries, many newspapers and magazines print articles about investing, and some devote themselves exclusively to the subject.

Later in this book, you'll learn about three ways in which the small investor can participate in the stock market with minimum risk, and find the names of organizations whose records of helping people learn about the market are outstanding.

Stock market investment is easy because you can investigate stocks in the privacy of your home, at any time of the day or night; and when you wish to make a purchase or a sale you have only to pick up the telephone and make a call, then put your check or stock certificate in the mail.

Furthermore, the stock certificate you receive when you buy common stock is small enough to fit in a drawer (although I recommend you use a safe deposit box in your bank or leave the certificate with your stockbroker) and won't raise your insurance rates.

Finally, investing in the stock market is easier because you can get started with as little as $20 a month; you don't have to wait until you've accumulated $10,000 or $100,000. In fact, sometimes, as you'll learn later, the person with a small amount of money can profit more easily than the one with hundreds of thousands to invest.

IT'S SAFE

Yes, I'm perfectly serious. Perhaps you're a senior citizen who lived through the stock market crash of 1929 and remembers people seeing their life savings wiped out, losing their homes, jumping out of windows.

If you're not that old, you've probably heard about all these things. "The stock market is dangerous. The stock market is for gamblers." You may have come across a book entitled, *Wall Street: The Other Las Vegas* by Nicholas Darvas (a man, incidentally, whose earlier book was *How I Made $2,000,000 in the Stock Market*), or one entitled *Wiped Out*, by a man who managed to lose an inheritance of $62,000 during one of the greatest bull market advances in history.

The stock market is not safe for small children, or people who won't pay attention to what they're doing. If you daydream while you're driving a car, pay no attention to stop lights, ignore other drivers, and watch scenery out of the side windows, then driving is unsafe; but normal, responsible drivers go right on driving every day, and certainly wouldn't if they didn't consider it relatively safe, Ralph Nader notwithstanding.

Investing in the stock market requires learning a few rules and acting sensibly, and thousands of people have found it a safe, reliable way of saving for the future. You can too.

One of the reasons it's safe is because you can always get your investment back; at any rate, most of it. Even if another crash like that of 1929 were to take place, there would be time to get out with most of your funds intact. Some people did at that time. The very fact that such a disaster occurred once should make you wary of holding on in the face of steadily dropping prices and panic in the streets. True, you might have to take a small loss to get out, but there's no excuse today for people losing everything in the market. It's the most liquid investment you can hold.

In a severe recession, banks may close their doors temporarily or fail. In a depression, you may not be able to dispose of your real estate at any price; there are simply no buyers for it. Rare books, collectibles, art and antiques are all difficult to sell when no one can afford to purchase anything but food.

But your stocks can be sold. The specialists on the exchanges are there for that very purpose. Even in 1929, opportunities existed to sell at a small loss, or even a profit, and get out of the market. People ignored them. Speculation had been so wild for so long that many people had very little cash in the market; they were borrowing heavily from their brokers. The margin rate (see Glossary) was as low as 10 percent at that time, and some were in debt for millions of dollars. When the first break came, instead of getting out, many of them added to their margin and made the final collapse even worse.

In October 1929 the market peaked at 381, as indicated by the Dow Jones Industrial Average. The plunge began on October 24, and dropped more or less steadily for the rest of the year. Then, in the spring of 1930, the market rallied and rose from 196 to 294, almost 100 points. People could have sold out then, and recouped some of their losses. Some did, in fact. Others didn't; they believed the market was going to go back up—in spite of numerous signs to the contrary—and so they watched their assets dwindle to a mere fraction of their pre-crash value by 1932.

The causes of the crash need not concern you here. The chances of it happening again are small, especially with the safeguards since enacted by the Securities and Exchange Commission, one of which is tighter margin requirements. Nevertheless, you need to know what to look for and how and when to act on knowledge that's available to everyone all the time.

Completely safe? No, nothing is completely safe. Not driving your car, crossing the street, or even taking a bath. (More people die in their bathtubs every year than are killed in airplane accidents.) As a pundit once said, "Don't take life too seriously; you'll never get out of it alive!" But if you have savings to invest, are reasonably careful, and follow the principles in this book, the stock market is one of the safer places to put your money.

IT'S FUN

Like easy, "fun" is a relative word. One man's relaxation is another man's boredom; one woman's delight is another's despair. You may like camping out; I loathe it.

But if you've picked up this book, you must have some interest in the stock market and that's enough of a foundation to find investing exciting as well as rewarding.

I can speak only for myself and the people I know who also invest regularly, but we enjoy it immensely and we're not "workaholics." Those of us in investment clubs enjoy the camaraderie and social occasions. We enjoy learning about business and money matters. We like using our analytical prowess, investigating companies, determining if their common stocks should be bought, held, or sold. We find it exciting to watch our choices grow in value. We even learn lessons from them when they decline. To us, the few hours a month that we spend on our hobby are pleasant and relaxing. I think investing can be an intriguing adventure for everyone.

Finally, investing in the stock market is not just a selfish thing to do, in the hopes of increasing our personal wealth, or even staying ahead of inflation. By saving money, by providing capital for business, we're doing more than helping ourselves; we're helping untold thousands of others. Investment in America, to use a cliche of an earlier decade, is not just a rousing sentiment; it's becoming recognized as a necessity if the way of life we've come to enjoy and expect will continue.

There have been forty serious inflationary periods in recent world history. In thirty-eight of them, the solution was a drastic governmental change, takeover by a dictatorship and loss of freedom for the people. When that happens, it's true that inflation disappears, but so does opportunity.

The inhabitants of such a society are strictly regulated as to what they may buy, where they may live or work, how or if they may travel. There are no choices left to them anymore. They have no one to represent them and are not permitted to vote for their leaders, much less choose whether to invest their savings (if indeed they have any savings) in cattle, coins, or commodities.

One of the misconceptions which somehow flourishes today is that there is a limited amount of capital available, that if one person has a lot of it, many other people are thereby deprived. This is simply not so. Capital is merely the savings of millions of people— you and me—and as long as we have jobs and the opportunity to earn money, as long as inflation doesn't rob us of the opportunity to save some of that income over our daily expenses, as long as confiscatory taxes don't take away the results of our labors, we can invest that money in banks (which then lend it to people for homes, goods, and services) or in business (directly or indirectly) through the stock market, for building plants, producing the goods we want, and employing us and our neighbors.

Profit is not a dirty word. Profit is what's left over after expenses. After your paycheck is used to buy food, clothing, and shelter, you hope to have some money left over. That's profit. When you don't have that profit, you're not only unhappy and resentful, you're deprived of a legitimate means of improving your standard of living and participating in society.

Your employers have the same necessity for profit. If they don't have any money left over after the expenses of running the business, they can't increase your salary next year, they can't buy new equipment, they can't hire new workers, they can't pay interest to the shareholders who invested their money to build the plant in the first place, and they can't donate some of it toward charitable causes, anymore than you can.

I'm glad it's becoming fashionable again to believe in rewards for our hard work and in building a stronger economy, which, in the long run, helps everyone. Those of us who still manage to save a little out of our paychecks can do our part. By investing that little money in common stocks, which will strengthen American enterprise, we're not only helping ourselves; in the long run, we're helping maintain freedom. As little as $20 a month can do it.

Why You Should Do it Yourself 2

Prior to 1972 my investment experience consisted of the example related in the first chapter and the purchase of shares of stock in the company where my husband worked. Even with a stock purchase plan to which the company contributed, we managed to do very poorly and took a loss. With buying a home, raising children, starting our own business, and my free-lance writing, there never seemed enough time or money to consider investing in the stock market. Until 1972.

As you'll read in a later chapter, I started an investment club and began to study the stock market seriously. Eventually we made money, proving, to my satisfaction at least, that anyone can do it provided he or she is willing to devote a small amount of time. Again, let me stress that I am talking about only two to five hours a month.

When my club began to be successful, friends often asked to join, and when our membership was full, I suggested they start their own instead. Through word of mouth, people I didn't know heard of me and came to me with questions about investment clubs. I helped to start several, and often spoke and answered questions at their early meetings.

Then in April 1981, on the ninth anniversary of my investment club, when our true annual return on investment was 18.57 percent, *Money* magazine featured on its cover an investment advisor who had earned a return on investment of better than 41 percent for his clients. The remaining seven investment advisors who were included in the article, called "master stock pickers," did not turn in as good a performance, however. Their returns on investment ranged from 13 percent to 25 percent, with the performance of four of them worse than that of our club.

Thrilled that our club had beaten half of these professionals, I read on and discovered that they based their calculations on a five-year period, not, as in the case of my club, on a nine-year period. They had not included the bear market of 1972–1974, one of the worst in recent history. Using my club's figures for the same five years as the "master stock pickers," I found we had earned an impressive 35.5 percent, beating all but one!

I wrote a letter about my club's success to *Money* magazine, which was published in their June issue. Then my phone began to ring and the rest, as they say, is history. Our club was interviewed and mentioned in the September issue of that magazine in an article about investment clubs; we were interviewed and our club was featured in the August issue of *50 Plus* magazine; and a story about the club was filmed by Home Box Office for a program which appeared on national television four times during the month of October. I was asked to speak at other club meetings and at the San Francisco Council of the National Association of Investment Clubs (N.A.I.C.), was deluged with requests from people who wanted to join my club, and helped several more new ones to start.

This book would not have been written if my enthusiasm about the investment club movement had not resulted in that letter to the editor. Suddenly, thanks to the publicity, I became an "expert," and my husband—and others—pointed out that I had no more excuses for not writing my own stock market book.

My point in mentioning all this is not to try to impress you but to show that any club, any individual, can probably do the same thing; that ordinary people can do as well or better than investment advisors.

Jerry Edgerton, in an article in the December 1983 issue of *Money*, reports, "Members of the National Association of Investment Clubs . . . have done more than twice as well over the past ten years as have the managers of the pension portfolios of 625 of the nation's largest banks."

Although I feel that the record of my club and the thousands of other clubs that are members of the N.A.I.C. is substantial proof that you don't need "experts" in order to make money in the stock market, an examination of investment advisors of all kinds may make this more evident.

INVESTMENT COUNSELORS

If you have $100,000 to invest, you don't need to "do it yourself;" you can go to an "investment counselor." Most of them will take your money, invest it as they see fit, and charge you 0.5 percent (payable quarterly) on the total value of your account, or a minimum of $2,000. If you're lucky enough to hire the man who made over 41 percent for his clients, and if he continues to perform so spectacularly, you won't need this book.

As $100,000 has dwindled in significance due to inflation, many counselors won't take accounts of that size any more, preferring that you invest at least $250,000. (That's a quarter of a million dollars!)

Even with that substantial investment, you may not find a good counselor. One very highly respected investment counselor in San Francisco refuses to take any new clients. The only time he considers it is when one of his present customers dies, and then the family of the deceased gets first chance. Another very successful investment counselor dropped his entire roster in 1970 and now invests only for himself.

But you don't have $250,000 to invest, do you? Or even $100,000, or $10,000? We're talking about sums you can spare from the weekly paycheck, sums as small as $20 a month. Can you get someone else to invest such a small amount for you and relieve you of the responsibility of doing it yourself? Probably not.

At one time there was a plan, entitled "Monthly Investment Program," or M.I.P., in which you could invest small amounts—as little as $40 a month, I believe—in a portfolio of stocks. This was started in the early sixties, but one doesn't hear of it anymore.

Today, the only brokerage which has such a plan is Merrill Lynch, Pierce, Fenner & Smith. Or you can join the N.A.I.C.'s Low-Cost Plan. In both of these cases, which will be described later in this book, you must make the decision yourself about which stocks to buy, so you're not relieved of that responsibility.

STOCKBROKERS

That you can get advice or portfolio management from a stockbroker is a delusion, especially if you invest only small amounts of money. Some of them may try to sell you a mutual fund, or turn you away. Like an investment counselor, the registered representative prefers to work with larger portfolios. Brokers have a legitimate reason for this; it makes more money for them, and their livelihood depends on making large commissions on many trades. The small investor can't hope to get much help from that quarter, therefore; with only a limited number of hours in the day, your broker must spend them producing the greatest income.

Brokers don't wish to harm you by ignoring or neglecting you. Certainly, if you have a small account at a brokerage and ask a specific question about a specific stock or industry, they will give you honest, helpful answers. But don't expect the brokerage to call you about a new opportunity that may mean great appreciation for your account; they're too busy calling people with more money. Likewise the people at the brokerage won't call you to advise selling a stock you already own; there's simply no time for it.

As for the value of their advice (if you do get it), there are wide variations. A broker depends on the stock analysts in the firm's research department and, as in most occupations, there are good analysts and bad ones. Furthermore, analysts may change jobs, so that the brokerage house which benefitted from an expert one year may suffer without him or her the next. Analysts even joke about their own research, saying, "In a good market you don't need it, and in a bad market you don't want it."

In a December 1984 article in *Money* it was reported that a survey of the stocks making up the Dow Jones Industrial Average revealed that during 1973-1983 you would have made three times as much by buying the stocks the analysts expected to have low earnings growth as by buying those they expected to do well.

Analysts, being human, can make the same errors as lay people. They may fall in love with stocks instead of looking at them objectively or succumb to peer pressure.

Brokers have one problem, in fact, that an individual investor will never experience: the need to report favorably on some stocks— right or wrong—rather than risk losing an investment banking customer. In 1982 an analyst at one New York brokerage removed a certain stock from the brokerage's recommended list and that company took its next public offering to another firm.

In addition, analysts may be forced to spend the majority of their time on companies that their institutional investors prefer; this could result in missed opportunities for the small investor.

Institutions, because of their huge sums of money, must invest in large corporations. Yet, the American Association of Individual Investors reports that in the past fifty years, you would have earned almost 100 percent more on your money by investing in the smallest 20 percent of companies listed on the New York Stock Exchange than in the largest companies. And it is these smaller companies which are generally popular with individual investors.

Consider, too, that individual investors accounted for 50 percent of trading volume in 1962. Today, institutions do 70 percent of the trading, and another 20 percent is done by professionals, leaving only 10 percent for individuals. Is it any wonder brokers ignore us?

MUTUAL FUNDS

"What about mutual funds?" you ask. "Won't they take small amounts of money and manage it for me?"

"Mutual funds" are investment companies and are regulated by the Securities and Exchange Commission. There are two types of investment companies, "closed-end" and "open-end." The shares of closed-end companies are traded on exchanges just like any other securities and you buy them from a broker.

Open-end investment companies are what we usually mean when we use the term mutual fund, and these are sold directly by the company or broker. They are called open-end because, unlike the closed-end fund, the capitalization changes. The public is permitted to buy into the fund at any time by paying the current asset value per share of the portfolio of stocks owned by the fund. The public may also sell at any time and will receive a sum equal to the number of shares held multiplied by the current asset value.

Most mutual funds require a minimum investment of $1,000, although some will accept deposits of $500; there are now over two thousand mutual funds to choose from. Finding the right mutual fund could be as demanding as determining which stock to buy. A mutual fund, like an investment counselor, will charge you a fee, as well as subtracting the cost of buying and selling shares over the year.

There are two basic kinds of open-end mutual funds, "no load" and "load." The load is the up-front sales charge, usually 8.5 percent, and it comes out of your deposit, so that you actually have less money invested than your initial payment. There is no charge, however, when you sell. No-load funds don't require this initial percentage, although they, too, charge an annual management fee of 0.5 percent and subtract commission costs for buying and selling.

A relatively new phenomenon is the "low-load" fund, usually a former no-load that now charges 1 to 3 percent up front. Other no-loads are assessing "exit" fees of 1 or 2 percent when you cash out.

Another method of charging fees is called the "12b-1" plan (from a 1980 Securities and Exchange Commission rule). A fund with such a plan usually charges no up-front sales fee but is allowed to use assets, instead of its annual fee, to pay for advertising and other expenses. If you already own shares in a mutual fund and want to know if this is the case, check the prospectus under the heading Distribution Plan or Distribution Charges.

Studies have shown, by the way, that on the average the fees charged have no bearing on performance, low-load or no-load funds doing as well as the others.

Benefits offered by mutual funds, besides a relatively low initial deposit, are: liquidity (you can redeem your shares for cash on short notice), diversification (investing in the shares of many companies and industries to spread risk), and professional management.

I'll take up these three points one at a time. Liquidity, or the ability to sell quickly, is not exclusive to funds. If you pay attention to the stock market, you can normally get out when circumstances dictate, regardless of whether you invest personally or through a mutual fund. It's certain that, if conditions deteriorate, no one from the mutual fund will write or telephone you suggesting that now would be a good time to sell! In other words, you must pay attention, even if your money is in a mutual fund.

As for diversification, there are two sides to this subject. While it's true that spreading your capital among many companies reduces risk, so that you don't lose it all if one of them collapses, it's also true that you reduce possible appreciation, because an average portfolio gives you merely average results.

A few successful investors put all their money in one stock which they feel has good prospects and then, if it fails to perform according to their expectations, get out with only a small loss and look for another one. This is the Mark Twain approach, as it was he who said, "Put all your eggs in one basket, and *watch* the basket!"

Professional management is judged, in the last analysis, by the results achieved by the funds. Many studies (including the famous one by the Wharton School of the University of Pennsylvania during the sixties) have shown that the funds have done no better (and in many cases worse) than the Dow Jones Industrial

Average, the Standard & Poor's 500, or other market averages. In fact, at one point the funds were performing so poorly and the cry of "Why can't you at least do as well as the averages?" was so pervasive that new funds appeared devoted specifically to buying the companies that made up these averages. And you can now buy shares of mutual funds which do not buy stocks at all, but buy shares of other mutual funds.

Every year in its last August issue, *Forbes* magazine rates the performance of mutual funds. Of over 700 funds studied in 1981, only 16 achieved a growth rate of at least 10 percent per year for the period December 1968 through November 1980 (142 months). The highest rate achieved among diversified stock funds was 13.9 percent. Investment clubs which are members of the National Association of Investment Clubs showed an increase of 21.12 percent for the time period of 123 months ending April 1981.

In 1984, mutual funds holding stocks showed a loss of 4.5 percent, whereas the Standard & Poor's 500 stock index rose 4.8 percent.

If you're even moderately acquainted with the stock market, you've heard the story that one can do better than most professional money managers by simply throwing darts at the page of stock tables. Well, in May 1981, the *New York Daily News* suggested such a contest, pitting Robert Stovall of Dean Witter Reynolds, Raymond DeVoe of Bruns Nordeman Rea, Michael Metz of Oppenheimer and Co., and William LeFevre of Purcell Graham & Co., against ten reporters provided with darts.

The reporters threw one dart each and ten stocks were thus chosen for an imaginary investment of $30,000. This "pretend" portfolio was held intact, whereas the professionals could buy and sell as many times as they wished with their make-believe $30,000.

At contest's end, June 30, the newspaper reporters' "choices" had gained 3.4 percent, outperforming three out of the four experts. Only Stovall's had risen, a handsome 26 percent.

Even if you manage to choose the exceptional, high-performing fund of last year, there is no guarantee it will do well next year. *Money* magazine's "Fund Watch" column frequently shows that a fund which ranks 2nd this year was 156th last year, or one that was 1st has dropped to 4th.

Although regulated by the Securities and Exchange Commission (S.E.C.), there are many cases of conflict of interest or practices among some mutual funds that would seem detrimental to the average investor. For example, many brokerage houses have their own funds, and therefore, the broker has a natural interest in selling that rather than another that might be better for your particular needs, or have a higher rate of return.

Additionally, mutual fund managers may tend to place their orders with brokers who offer them the best rates, and therefore those fund managers might "return the favor" by buying stocks recommended by the brokers, not necessarily those with the best growth possibilities.

Other questionable practices that may be followed by some funds (particularly small funds without adequate research staffs) are relying on tips and rumors or succumbing to the "herd instinct" by buying and selling shares in unison with other funds.

As in any business, there is the risk of outright fraud or illegality. Fortunately such instances are rare; however in April 1981, one mutual fund was liquidated for that reason.

When a mutual fund does well, it attracts many new investors, and this very popularity can create a problem; the fund may find it more difficult than the small investor to turn a profit. Large funds with millions or even billions to invest can't move in and out of the market as easily as someone with smaller sums at stake. For this reason mutual funds and other institutions with large sums of money are virtually forced into buying shares of the largest corporations in the country, those with many millions of shares outstanding.

Buying huge amounts of the stock of a smaller company may increase the price, so that the fund purchases the latter shares at somewhat higher prices than the earlier ones; correlatively, to sell 100,000 or more shares of a smaller company's stock may depress its price, so that by the time all have been placed, the fund will receive less than the price at which it wished to sell.

For these reasons, some mutual funds and other large investors must forego investing in some small, new companies that might have the potential for phenomenal future growth.

INVESTMENT ADVISORS

You may ask, "Suppose I'm willing to do the actual investing myself, but I don't want to do the research; are there advisors who will tell me what to buy and when?"

Yes, there are investment advisory services, whose annual fee may be from $150 to several thousand dollars a year, and there are investment newsletters costing somewhat less.

The advisory services usually have newsletters of their own, in which they make recommendations to buy or sell; some of them have made good suggestions. The suspicion remains, however, that not only do advisory services have the same drawbacks as mutual funds regarding possible conflict of interest, but such services must spend much of their time and energy maintaining their clients from year to year and devote minimal amounts to research.

Choosing investment advisors is akin to choosing a mutual fund; there are too many. And, unlike a mutual fund, it's sometimes difficult to find statistics showing their results.

The *Hulbert Financial Digest* (to which you can subscribe for $135 a year, as of this writing) reports on the success or failure of newsletters in picking stocks. In early 1984, the *Digest* examined the portfolios suggested by seventy-four investment newsletters and found that 75 percent of them failed to do as well as the Dow Jones Industrial Average. Worse, half of them failed to do better than the rate of return on risk-free U.S. Treasury bills. At the end of 1984, the newsletter which ranked first was found to have been last in 1983! This digest, by the way, analyzes only a handful of the available newsletters, so there is the possibility that some good ones may inadvertently be overlooked.

One investment advisor, Joseph Granville, made major headlines the first week of January 1981, when the Dow Jones Industrial Average stood at 1004, by sending telegrams to his clients advising them to "sell everything." Reacting promptly, they sent the Dow Jones Industrial Average down 23 points the next day. However, the market turned around quickly and rallied, closing higher the very next week. It went over 1020 in April and again in June. There was no such warning, apparently, in early August, when the market began its four-week 100-point plunge.

One of the important things to know is that anyone—even you—can become an investment advisor. So long as you have no criminal record and can fill in a simple form provided by the S.E.C., you can form your own advisory company, solicit clients and even manage their money. You don't even have to bother with this registration if you meet the following qualifications: you only write a newsletter, your subscribers are mainly in your own state, and you handle none of their money.

Some years ago, a publication called *The Trading Floor* appeared on newsstands in New York City, giving market advice and selling for fifty cents an issue. It turned out to be written entirely by a 19-year-old boy whose mother helped him collate and staple the pages on her kitchen table. The S.E.C. registration form had not required him to state his age. Still, people spend an estimated $150 million a year subscribing to newsletters.

OTHER SOURCES OF ADVICE

A popular television program, "Wall Street Week," hosted by the charming Louis Rukeyser, is informative and interesting, but surveys have shown that you probably can't make money in the market by buying on Monday anything recommended on the show the previous Friday evening. These stocks rise about 2 percent that day, and will usually rise another 0.1 percent during the next eleven days. Six weeks later, however, they've dropped back to their original prices. There's nothing wrong with the advice given by the panelists; it's just that by the time they appear on the program, the stocks they've suggested may have already risen in price.

"How about going straight to the top, the company itself?" You can write or telephone to a firm which interests you, asking them specific questions regarding their stock. They're forbidden, however, by law, to give you "insider information" not available to everyone else. In fact, they're not permitted to profit by such information themselves. And if you think an officer of the firm will tell you anything but the most favorable news about the company, you're more naive than is good for you.

While this chapter was under revision, an item in *Time* magazine caught my attention because it described how a London investment analyst allowed an English sheep dog named William to choose its own investments. The owner read a list of stocks, pausing after each for a short time. If William barked after a name, the stock of that company was purchased. Since 1973 the dog's "choices" have proved so profitable that his portfolio has increased from $2,500 to $109,000! The analyst began the experiment to prove that a dog could do better at picking stocks than most money managers; his results seem to have proved both his point and mine about the quality of outside advice.

It would seem that the old saying, "If you're so smart, how come you're not rich?" is nowhere more applicable than in the stock market. Cheap advice is often worth just what you pay for it, and even advice that costs you dearly may prove to be little better. The really smart people seem to be busy making themselves rich. You will simply have to learn to do the same. After all, no one will ever be more concerned about your money than you!

In the following chapters you'll learn where to find the basic tools of investing and how to go about it for yourself.

Basics–What Are Common Stocks? 3

Although I've assumed a certain basic knowledge of the stock market on your part, it may be helpful to cover some rudimentary aspects of the subject at this time and to explain some terms with which you may not be completely familiar.

It's one thing to know the stock market exists and, in a general way, to know how it operates, but quite another to feel comfortable with your knowledge and able to converse with your broker, your fellow investment club members, and those who may ask you questions once they know you're an investor.

ISSUING STOCK

To begin at the beginning, let's talk about how stocks originate. A small business—one operating out of a home, for example—might wish to expand into a regular store or factory, hire employees, and buy more raw material, but finds itself without sufficient capital for the undertaking. A bank might lend it money, but if the loan officers don't possess the same faith in the idea and in the ability of the owners to make the business profitable they might refuse. Friends or relatives might also lend money to the owners for start-up purposes, but it's been said that the quickest way to lose a friend is to borrow or lend money.

Stocks and Bonds

A third alternative is to incorporate the business and "go public" by selling stocks and bonds in the corporation to the general public. Since we're not going to discuss bonds in detail in this book, I will merely say that a bond is a type of loan made to a corporation, with a fixed rate of interest, just as if the money had been borrowed from a bank.

Stocks, on the other hand, are shares in the company. The person who owns stocks will share in the good or bad fortune of that business. If the business does well, the stockholder may receive high dividends (similar to interest on a bond or loan) or the price of the stock may appreciate, so that the stockholder can sell it for more than he or she paid for it and realize a capital gain.

Another important difference between bonds and stocks is that the bondholder is merely a lender, with no say in the running of the company. A stockholder, on the other hand, being a kind of partner in the enterprise, has an interest in the business. The value of a stockholder's shares rises and falls depending upon the operations of the company and he can vote on pertinent matters according to the number of shares held.

Common and Preferred Stocks

There are two kinds of stock, common and preferred. We are not going to deal with preferred stocks in this book, but I do want to explain the difference to you. Generally, smaller amounts of preferred stock are offered to the public, and their price does not vary as much as that of the common. This is because preferred stockholders get a fixed dividend rate rather than one that fluctuates with the fortunes of the company. Preferred stockholders, like bondholders, have no voting rights.

The advantage to preferred stocks lies in the fact that should the company have a bad year the preferred stockholders would receive dividends before the common stockholders. Additionally, should the company fail and go out of business, the owners of preferred stock would get preferential treatment when the remaining assets were distributed.

In order to issue stock, the company contacts an investment banker or broker who underwrites the stock; that is, a broker buys stock from a corporation and sells it to the public for a profit. The initial price of the stock is fixed at this time, but never again. From then on the price of shares in the company varies depending on the price the public is willing to pay for it.

STOCK EXCHANGES

Since our imaginary company is small, its stock will be traded "over the counter"; that is, it will not be listed on an exchange, such as the New York Stock Exchange or American Stock Exchange. There is, however, an organization, the National Association of Securities Dealers, that does list such stocks and gives quotes on them based on the past buying and selling experience of those shares. The public has simply to call a regular stockbroker and buy them, just as if they were listed on an exchange.

One of the interesting historical notes about the stock market is that the New York Stock Exchange was founded in 1792 by a group of businessmen who met under a buttonwood tree on Wall Street for the purpose of trading securities (stocks and bonds) issued by corporations doing business in the new country or by the United States Government to pay for the Revolutionary War.

The American Stock Exchange was formed later, and is sometimes known as the "Curb"; the New York Stock Exchange is sometimes called the "Big Board." There are other stock exchanges besides those in New York, such as the Pacific Coast Stock Exchange, Boston Exchange, Philadelphia Exchange, and some in Canada. Knowing these things is not necessary for successful investing, but merely acquaints you with some of the terminology. There are some fascinating books about the history of Wall Street, which you may wish to delve into some day. If you visit New York, or have a stock exchange in your own city, you'll certainly find touring one to be both interesting and informative.

Listing on one of the exchanges is done by meeting the requirements of that particular exchange. These requirements concern such things as value of the company, number of shares outstanding, number of stockholders, and after-tax earnings.

Because of these requirements, investors often feel that they wish to purchase only those stocks that are listed on well-known exchanges, and it is true that those stocks will usually have a larger following and stronger financial base than unlisted stocks. However, as we'll see later, unlisted stocks should not be excluded from consideration by a small investor or an investment club. Other criteria that help to determine whether a stock should be purchased will be discussed later.

The only people who can trade stocks on an exchange are the members, and members must buy "seats" in order to do so. Some, not all, members trade for the general public; but all brokerage houses are members of the exchanges.

When you call your broker to buy or sell stocks, he or she transfers your order—by computer these days—to the exchange member for the brokerage house, who then executes the order on the exchange floor. There's a great deal of talk about computerizing the entire process and thereby doing away with exchanges entirely, but so far that hasn't come to pass.

STOCKBROKERS

Since you aren't permitted to buy and sell stock yourself, getting a broker to do it for you is a necessary first step to investing. Whether you are an individual investor or a member of an investment club, you must approach a brokerage house and find a registered representative who will execute your orders. He or she will want to know something about you, your financial goals (whether you wish to invest for capital appreciation or income and how much risk you feel comfortable with), and how you will manage the account. Since most transactions are made with a telephone call and can sometimes involve large sums of money, it's important that both customer and broker trust one another.

The broker can be a good source of information about stocks and the market; but as we've said earlier, the broker's time is valuable, and you ought not to waste it with unnecessary questions. In fact, if you use a discount broker in order to save on commission costs, you'll find they won't ask questions about your goals or give you any information or advice.

Sources of Information

To get information, read newspapers. Besides the *Wall Street Journal,* every large metropolitan daily carries stock pages, listing at least the New York Stock Exchange companies, and usually the American Stock Exchange (Amex) and some over-the-counter stocks as well. In addition, the business pages carry articles about local and national companies; and magazines, services such as Value Line and Standard & Poor's, and books are helpful. These will be discussed in detail in a later chapter.

Today, with personal computers in so many homes, a further way to obtain financial information is through database services such as The Source, CompuServe, or Dow Jones Information Retrieval.

Specialists

Before concluding the discussion of the exchanges we ought to touch briefly on the "specialist." This is an exchange member who is assigned certain stocks in which he or she is expected to "make a market." This means that the specialist does the buying and selling for those stocks, and if you want to sell one of these stocks and there is no other purchaser at the time, the specialist will buy it.

Conversely, if you want to buy and there are no sellers, the specialist will sell from his or her own supply. The specialist tries to match buyers and sellers equitably and to run an "orderly market," that is, one with no wide gaps between prices asked by the sellers and offers made by the buyers.

At one time there were additional brokers involved in stock transactions, the "odd-lot dealers." An odd lot is a number of shares less than 100. (One hundred shares is called a "round lot.") In the past, if you wished to purchase an odd lot, your broker had to go through the odd-lot dealer and arrange for it, and you would be charged a small fee for this service. Today, however, most brokerage houses perform this service themselves and don't charge the customer any more than the usual fee for buying stock.

Discount Brokers

With the deregulation of the industry a few years ago, costs of buying and selling stock changed. We've already discussed discount brokers, but you may be wondering about the differences between them and regular brokers. Before deregulation, brokers charged specific rates for any particular transaction based upon the amount of money and the number of shares involved. Controversy arose, however, because institutions, such as pension funds or other groups with large amounts to invest, felt discriminated against. It takes about the same effort on the part of the broker to handle a transaction involving thousands of dollars as it does to handle one involving hundreds of dollars, yet the commissions on the larger transactions were much higher. Since deregulation, brokers are free to charge whatever they think is fair to handle transactions. In actual practice, although transaction costs to other customers have changed little, most brokers give better prices to institutional investors.

With deregulation and the new freedom to set rates, discount brokers came on the scene. They could offer substantially lower rates to those institutional investors who, because they had research staffs of their own to evaluate stocks, didn't require such services from the broker. Anyone, not just institutional investors, is free to take advantage of these lower prices; but be aware of the nature of the service: it is strictly a buy-or-sell operation and no research, information, or other help will be given.

Since investment clubs, like institutions, do their own research and investigation into stocks, advice from the broker is probably unnecessary and discount brokers will save them money. As you'll learn later in this book, even an individual investor can become sufficiently knowledgeable about equities to forego a full-service broker for a discount broker.

MONEY MARKET FUNDS

The entire banking industry has been deregulated, and the changes are far-reaching. Banks are going into the brokerage business and regular brokers, whether discount or not, are free to offer interest on money held.

The money market fund is a recent phenomenon. Until about 1977, banks were permitted to pay only 5 or 5.5 percent on savings. Investors with large sums, however, could buy Certificates of Deposit, which at the time could only be bought in amounts of $100,000 or more. Money market funds sprang up to pool the small amounts of many investors to buy these CDs, as well as safe government securities, such as Treasury Bills.

Investment clubs can benefit greatly from brokers' money market funds. When contributions are received from club members, the money can be temporarily placed in the money market fund to earn interest until the members vote to buy stock with it. When stock is sold, the broker can deposit the money into the money market fund immediately after the transaction is completed, so that it begins to earn interest at once.

Naturally, this service is just as valuable for an individual investor, who may want to set aside investment money regularly or let funds earn interest between selling one stock and buying another.

Safety

It must be remembered that money market funds, whether in a brokerage house or bank, are not insured by the federal government. However, your account, just like savings accounts in banks or savings and loans, is protected. This is because all stockbrokers are members of the S.I.P.C., Securities Insurance Protection Corporation.

DIVIDENDS AND CAPITAL GAINS

Whether investing privately or through a club, an investor's primary purpose is to make money, and stocks provide two ways of doing this: through dividends and through capital gains.

Dividends, generally issued quarterly, are paid by most companies offering stock. This money, which will come to you in the form of a check from the company itself or from your broker, represents a form of interest on your investment. If you own shares of XYZ Corporation and it announces a twenty-five-cent quarterly dividend, you'll receive twenty-five cents for each share you own. This money can be reinvested or spent in any way you choose. If you paid $10 a share for the stock, you're getting a 10 percent yield on your investment.

On the other hand, when you sell the stock (provided you've held it long enough to qualify), whatever profit you make from its sale is considered "capital gains." The government taxes you differently on dividends (or interest) and capital gains. You may want to ask a tax consultant or other adviser about how to handle this on your income tax return. In the case of investment clubs, the treasurer's manual contains information about how to determine dividends and capital gains and report them to the members.

As stated earlier, your dividend checks will come to you either from the company itself or from your broker, depending on what arrangements you have made with the latter. Some clubs leave their stock certificates in "street name"; that is, in the name of the brokerage house. Your ownership of the stock is carried on their records, and when a dividend comes in to the brokerage, it's credited to your account.

Both dividends and capital gains are important in investing, and will be discussed in more detail in a later chapter.

STOCK CERTIFICATES

To keep your own stock certificates, simply instruct the broker to send them to you at the time you make the purchase. If you go this route, you'll want to have a safety deposit box in a bank in which to store them, as they're valuable and should not be left where they can be lost or destroyed.

The disadvantage of this, aside from the cost of renting the box, is that you (or in the case of an investment club, someone who is appointed to the task) must keep the key to the box and deposit the certificates, then take them out and send them to the broker when the stock is subsequently sold. Most small investors and investment clubs, however, do not consider it a problem, and they request their own certificates and keep them in a safety deposit box.

When you own stock in a company, several things can happen. You will receive annual reports, notices of stockholders' meetings, and other communications from the company. You might receive dividend checks. There are several other possibilities—stock dividends, rights, and stock splits—you should know about.

Stock Dividends

Instead of cash dividends, you may receive stock dividends, which are additional shares of stock issued to you in proportion to how many shares you already own. Remember, stock dividends are issued in lieu of cash dividends.

Rights

You may also be offered "rights." These, too, have value, since they generally allow you to buy shares at a lower-than-market price. For example, if the stock is selling at $10 a share, you'll be given the "right" to buy it at $8 a share. Rights have a short life span, and you should sell them (through your broker) or exercise them before they expire.

Stock Splits

The company in which you own stock may "split" its stock, offering shareholders, for example, two shares for every one they currently hold. Most splits are two for one, but there are also three-for-one splits, five-for-four splits, or splits in any other possible combination. Should this happen, don't think that your assets have suddenly increased; they haven't. Although you now own more shares than before, each share is worth less, giving you approximately the same total value.

Companies split their stock for various reasons. Some feel that lower-priced shares attract more investors, and split the stock whenever they think the price has become too high. Since the split is announced in newspapers, it also creates some publicity and attention for the company and may result in higher prices.

TAKEOVERS AND TENDER OFFERS

When one company wants to merge with another, officers of the first company make a "Tender offer" to the management of the second (object) company, which is then presented to that company's stockholders. A "takeover", on the other hand, is usually not so friendly. In this case, the acquiring company will offer stockholders a price for their shares above that prevailing in the market place at that time, hoping to gain control of the company thereby.

Takeovers can sometimes be profitable for investors. The price of the stock of the object company may rise dramatically. You must be nimble, however, because the price can drop just as rapidly. If the offer is withdrawn, or if, as in the case of Saul Steinberg and Walt Disney Productions in 1984, the officers buy the raider out, you'll not only see the price deteriorate, but the company, now saddled with an unexpected expense, may be worth less.

The practice of attempting unfriendly takeovers, which occasionally end like the one at Disney, has been nicknamed "greenmail," as some investors have likened it to "blackmail played with a lot of money."

Of course the persons or firms attempting the takeover may be unsuccessful. They may end up with neither the company nor a premium for their shares. The object company may do its own buying, making itself still larger and thwarting the efforts of the pirates. Or it may sell off the particular product that attracted the interest. If that happens, the stock price will drop, and the "green-mailers" will have paid a higher than current price for the shares they accumulated.

Additional reading, which I always recommend, will make these terms more familiar to you; but I hope you've absorbed enough now to understand the remaining chapters.

What Is an
Investment Club?

4

Having read this far, you know that I advocate ownership of common stocks for everyone. It's a myth that you have to have lots of money to "play the market." It is true that the more money you have, the more you can earn with it, but it's equally true that unless you get started with some program to increase capital, you will never have more than you do today. Faced with the high rates of inflation we saw in the seventies and which may return, the fact is you could have far less buying power in the future if you don't do something constructive now. To my mind, joining or starting an investment club is a wonderful way for millions of people to accumulate capital for a better life or more secure future. The sooner you start, the better.

THE INVESTMENT CLUB IDEA

Investment clubs have been active in the United States for about eighty years, the oldest known club having begun in Texas in 1898. Early clubs seem to have been more social than educational, however. In 1940 an investment club in Detroit became the model for the type of club most popular today. Its founder advocated learning as much as possible about the investment process and adopted the three principles that still guide N.A.I.C. member clubs:

31

(1) Invest every month. (2) Reinvest all dividends. (3) Invest in growth companies.

A national association of investment clubs was proposed in 1949, but it wasn't until 1951 that it finally took shape, with that first modern club, The Mutual Investment Club of Detroit, and three other Michigan clubs as its first members.

Since then, the investment club movement has spread across the country and overseas, with the establishment of the World Federation of Investment Clubs in 1960. Twenty years later, in 1980, this worldwide movement adopted a series of principles called the "Investor's Magna Charta," proclaiming that investors in a company, no less than management and labor, have rights. The complete document, as well as additional information about the investment club movement, can be found in the N.A.I.C. *Investors' Manual. Better Investing* Magazine, published by the N.A.I.C., is probably the largest magazine in the world devoted exclusively to investor education.

This education can lead to more than a future nest egg. Worldwide financial complexity increases constantly, and understanding it can help in all family decisions. Many club members find their new awareness of finance leads to advancement in their jobs. Women, who (in this country at least) tend to live longer than men, find this knowledge invaluable if left alone in later years to handle their husbands' estates.

Individuals can join the National Association of Investment Clubs, subscribe to its magazine, and take advantage of all the other benefits of membership. This approach will be discussed later in this book; nevertheless I believe that joining with others in an investment club offers the surest, most enjoyable way to profit.

One of the advantages is that you can invest in the market with very small sums of money, as little as $20 a month. If this is all you ever invest, you may, perhaps, not become a millionaire in your lifetime; but the result of your investment could come in handy for a fancy vacation in the future or could help to put your children through college or provide you an additional income for your retirement years. And you will have achieved one or more of these worthwhile goals by investing money you never missed.

If your club becomes successful or you find yourself with larger sums for investing, you can if you wish invest more than $20 a month in your club or start a second or third club or use the capital—and the expertise—thus acquired for personal investing. Many investment club members have done all these things.

Even if each member of the club contributes only $20 a month, with fifteen members (the recommended number) you will have

$300 to invest every month. If you had to wait until you had $300 of your own you might have to wait a long time to get started. But almost anyone can usually find $20 a month with which to begin an investment program that might provide his or her family with many future luxuries.

By pooling their resources in this way, the investment club members are able to approach a stockbroker with a sum they're not ashamed to mention and the added realization that due to the continuing nature of their contributions similar sums will be invested regularly over many years. Most brokers who would turn away a private investor with only $300 to invest will take on an investment club, confident that the ongoing nature of the club will provide similar amounts at regular intervals. Our own club, starting with only fourteen members, was worth more than $50,000 ten years later, a respectable growth record.

Statistics show some clubs did much better than that. The N.A.I.C. keeps records of member clubs, and every year reports on their progress, with the best being listed in the pages of its monthly magazine, *Better Investing*.

At the end of 1983, 241 clubs reported their results. The average age of the clubs was nine and a half years and the compound annual earnings rate was 27.8 percent. The results of the Standard & Poor's 500 for the same period was 16.9 percent. In only three of the last twenty-three years have the clubs' earnings rates fallen below the averages.

Not all investment clubs are members of the N.A.I.C. It's estimated there may be over 20,000 clubs in the United States with over 300,000 members. N.A.I.C. member clubs totaled 14,000 at the organization's peak in 1970. It dropped to a low of 3,500, but now stands at 6,000, with a total membership of 112,230 persons. Throughout the years, about two and a half million people have been in the N.A.I.C.'s programs at one time or another.

The reason for this fluctuation is found in the nature of the stock market itself. When the Dow Jones Industrial Average makes new highs, when the volume traded on the New York Stock Exchange breaks previous records, people invest in record numbers. Then new clubs form. But when fortune no longer smiles, when most stock prices are dropping, and members see their capital dwindle, they become pessimistic and clubs may fold.

Not all clubs report their statistics to the N.A.I.C. Less successful clubs are naturally reluctant to broadcast this information, so the record may be slightly slanted in favor of the better results. But the fact that 241 clubs can outperform the averages and many mutual funds, year after year, ought to encourage beginners that there is reason for optimism.

Consider this: the average investment club member spends about five hours per month working on his or her investments; yet many have done better than professionals who spend eight hours a day at it, five days a week, twenty days a month!

SOME OUTSTANDING CLUBS

The Value Line Investment Survey selected certain clubs for recognition—and a cash award—in 1982, and their choices were outstanding evidence that investment clubs can outperform "experts."

Hi Lo Investment Club of Grand Rapids, Michigan, although only twenty-eight months old at the time, topped the list with an annual earnings rate of 70.3 percent. Two years later, now fifty-one months old and having survived the lackluster performance of the market in 1984, it won second place, with 26 percent growth.

Interestingly, this club was the second for many of its members. The first closed its books after twenty-one years of operation because many of the members were nearing retirement age. Needless to say, their retirement is sweeter for the hefty profits their club generated. The newer club is no slouch either, and although the computer industry stocks the club profited from have since dipped and been sold, they still own a few good ones. Their current portfolio, limited to nine issues at the moment, is diversified with stock from A.T. & T. and T.G.I. Friday. They've also made money with Herman Miller Company, an office furniture manufacturer.

Meanwhile, an eight-year-old club in San Jose, California, won first prize in 1984 with a record 45 percent increase.

In second place in 1982 was the Highlander Investment Club of Holden, Massachusetts, which earned 45.7 percent over its lifetime of sixteen years. The original members of the club were part of a men's and women's bowling team, but had no difficulty switching from pins to profits. Their largest holding at the moment is in C. K. Lowes Company stock, which they've purchased several times over the past few years. Their average cost per share was a little over $9.00 and it's now worth $27.50.

Third-place club in 1982 hails from Minnesota and had compounded earnings of 33.5 percent in its almost three and a half years of operation.

In Ohio, the top club for the state in 1982 was P.A.I.D. (Professional Association of Investors of Defiance) with an average gain of 25.6 percent a year. This club, which was founded in 1972, also won the Value Line Survey in both 1975 and 1977, and was featured in "PM Magazine" and then on national television.

Their successes include purchases of I.B.M. stock for an average price of $76, now trading at $125; Wendy's, which went from about $5 to $17; H. J. Heinz, which went from less than $18 to over $55; and General Cinema, which went from under $16 to over $38.

A top club in Maryland earned 25 percent during four years; and another ten-year-old club in Houston, Texas, increased at the rate of 19.4 percent per year.

All these clubs report that they follow N.A.I.C. guidelines, usually are almost fully invested in the market, keeping very little cash, and use fundamental analysis to determine when to buy and sell stocks. The members come to the meetings armed with copies of the *Wall Street Journal, Barron's,* and the latest issue of *Better Investing,* as well as completed copies of the N.A.I.C. Stock Selection Guide, to present their stock recommendations to one another.

The Park Merced Investment Club near San Francisco began in 1966 with fifteen men and women who all lived in the Park Merced apartment complex and put in a total of $1,000; by 1981, with members continuing to invest $20 a month, it had grown to $78,000 and is currently worth over $93,000. After a lackluster performance in 1983, the club turned 1984 into a banner year as their portfolio advanced 70 percent.

One of the original members of the Park Merced club then started a second club for retired persons at the Center for Learning in Retirement (C.L.I.R.); to show that age is no barrier to market success, these fifteen men and women invested $15.00 a month and within two years saw their unit value at $21.30. Their winners more than compensated for a loss in I.B.M. stock, which they bought at $82 and sold at $56. One hundred shares of Sealectro stock on the American Stock Exchange cost them a little over $600 and eighteen months later were worth $2,218. In its third year of operation C.L.I.R. Investment Club was named top club of the year by the N.A.I.C., with an annual gain of 40.8 percent.

Another San Francisco club, Witches of Wall Street, made up of members of a local chapter of the American Association of University Women, got its start in 1982 and immediately had a winner by buying Apple Computer stock at $13 a share and selling it at $45.

Some Half Moon Bay, California, members of A.A.U.W. formed a club in 1979 which posted a 37 percent gain by 1983. Their shares of Ask Computer Systems, purchased at $16, split two for one and are now worth about $20 each. They too made money in Apple Computer stock, buying at $20.50 and selling at $58.50. They've had their share of "dogs", but their gains keep them ahead. As one member put it, "You don't have to be right 100 percent of the time; you only have to be right more than you're wrong!"

Share Growers Investment Club of Millbrae, California, attributes some of its success to the luck of starting the club just at the beginning of the bull market in 1982; but its founder obviously knew what she was doing, since she won fourth prize in the Standard & Poor's 500 Challenge contest which ended in May 1985. The club did very well with Wendy's International which went from $14.00 a share to over $18.00, and with Pik'n'Save, bought at $18.75 and sold at more than $33.

Futures Unlimited III is, you guessed it, the third club for a group of Hillsborough, California, women. The first club was liquidated with a gain after four years so that they could change their bookkeeping system. The second club was liquidated after almost twenty years, because some members had so much money in it that withdrawal might have meant hardship for the club.

The newest club has everyone starting off even again, investing $25 a month. Among their successes are I.B.M., bought at $70 and sold at $130, and Vendo stock, which they purchased because a friend's husband had just become president. That one went from $2.50 a share to $6.00 in less than a year. Advanced Micro Devices gave them a profit of almost $4,000.

A Camp Hill, Pennsylvania, club is proud to have outperformed the Standard & Poor's average for twenty-five years; and a club at the College of Wooster, Ohio, earned 37 percent on its investment since its founding twenty-eight years ago.

Finally, that oldest club, The Mutual Investment Club of Detroit, is still in business forty-five years later and is worth more than one and a half million dollars, in spite of cash withdrawals by its members of $400,000.

BETTER INVESTING

When a club joins the N.A.I.C., the monthly magazine *Better Investing* comes to each member's home address and provides ongoing education and information. Several stocks are usually mentioned in its pages every month, but one will always be profiled as the "Stock to Study" for that month. If club members did nothing but buy the stocks suggested there they would outperform the Dow Jones Industrial Average two-thirds of the time.

In the first twenty-seven years that the editors of *Better Investing* calculated the results, the choices of the "Stock to Study" beat the Average eighteen times. In the past twenty-five years, they have beaten it twenty times.

Additional help is available through other articles in each issue, as well as through its most popular feature, "The Repair Shop." In its columns, readers can learn of problems other clubs may be facing and the N.A.I.C. experts' advice.

Besides statistics about specific companies, the magazine discusses prospects for certain industries, the investment climate, both fundamental and technical analysis techniques, suggestions for adding or keeping club members, and ways to operate more efficiently. In addition, readers can learn of a "Model Portfolio" suggested by the association, which may be especially helpful to new clubs.

MORE N.A.I.C. HELP

As if all this weren't enough, the N.A.I.C. provides still more services. A club or an individual can subscribe to its advisory service, which gives specific recommendations.

Forms to use when studying stocks, such as the N.A.I.C.'s Stock Selection Guide, can be purchased at bargain prices. The forms make decisions easier as well as more likely to be successful. These forms will be more thoroughly discussed in later chapters.

Membership in the N.A.I.C. will cost your club $30 a year, plus $6 for each member. Your club will be given a $25,000 fidelity bond to protect you in case of theft or fraud, and you can purchase an additional one when the value of your portfolio exceeds that amount.

ACCOUNTING RECORDS

I also highly recommend sending for the *Accounting Manual* for your club's treasurer and any forms necessary to the N.A.I.C.-recommended method of keeping track of members' contributions and the value of the club.

Several clubs, including our own, didn't do this at first, assuming that each member would remain with the club and invest $20 per month regularly, thus owning an equal share. But as we've seen, the size of members' monthly contributions can vary.

The club treasurer will naturally be better informed about proper accounting procedures than other members, but each member should read the section in the *Investor's Manual* that gives an overview of the accounting procedures, not only to be sure the treasurer handles the job correctly, but also to prepare for the day he or she may be elected treasurer.

The *Treasurer's Manual* provides step by step guidance through the monthly record-keeping and annual tax statements and helps with other problems that may arise.

The advantages of using the N.A.I.C. method of accounting are many.

1. It has been thoroughly tested with thousands of clubs and has evolved over many years.
2. It provides for members to withdraw, or make partial withdrawals of, their money without undue hardship on the remaining members.
3. It provides for new members to join without having to invest a large initial sum to "catch up" to the others.
4. It allows for members to contribute more than $20 a month if they desire.
5. It assists members to handle tax liability at the end of each year. Let me emphasize here the essential nature of this procedure. All members of the club *must* report earnings or losses—as reported by the club treasurer—on their personal income tax returns. The president and treasurer should remind members at least once a year that this is mandatory.

Although clubs are sometimes disbanded after a few years, the lessons learned are never forgotten and continue benefitting the members long after they stop putting $20 into their club every month. In Chapter 5 I'll tell you exactly how to go about starting your own investment club, and in chapter 6 I'll discuss in detail some ideas that have helped clubs to prosper as well as some pitfalls to avoid.

Meanwhile here's that important address: National Association of Investment Clubs, 1515 E. Eleven Mile Road, Royal Oak, Michigan 48067.

How to Start Your Own Club

5

As I was writing this chapter, I had a telephone call from a woman who saw my picture and article about investment clubs in a local newspaper. She wanted to join my club, but I told her we had no vacancies and suggested she start her own.

"Oh," she said, "I wouldn't have the time to start a club."

As I've said, many callers have approached me about becoming members; therefore, this chapter begins by discussing the possibility of joining a club already in existence.

Most clubs limit membership to between ten and fifteen. They may have already reached the limit, and (like my own) may even have a waiting list. Occasionally there are openings in clubs. Theoretically, it should be possible to join one of them; but investing money brings out strong feelings in people, and they are understandably reluctant to allow a total stranger to join their circle. Therefore, the best method of approach is to cultivate a friend who is a member of an investment club. If you know such a person and would feel comfortable allowing him or her to have a voice in how your investment dollars are spent, by all means get in touch with that person and ask if you may join the club. Be prepared to be turned down, however.

If you're unsuccessful in your attempts to join an established club, then start your own. It has distinct advantages. In this way you'll have absolute control over who may become a member and how the club will operate. And it's not at all difficult, especially when the N.A.I.C. helps. Their *Investor's Manual* contains an excellent section on how to start a club. Once you've made the initial contact and invited people to discuss the idea, everyone works at it together.

So, how did I respond to the woman who asked to join my club, but said she didn't have time to start her own? I told her that if she had time to participate in a club, she had time to start one.

GETTING STARTED

My experience is typical. In February 1972, I read an article in my local newspaper about the N.A.I.C. and its member clubs. The clubs had just reported their results for the previous calendar year, and learning that the average club had outperformed the results of both the Dow Jones Industrial Average and the Standard and Poor's averages by a considerable margin impressed me.

The article gave a brief history of the N.A.I.C. and listed the three rules which they believed accounted for the success of these clubs. They were: (1) Invest regularly, regardless of whether you think the market is up or down. (2) Invest in growth companies. (3) Reinvest all dividends.

Before this, I had no idea the N.A.I.C. existed or that so many investment clubs took a commonsense approach to investing in the stock market. In my reading I had come across a reference to a group of apparently bored and wealthy women, who formed an "investment club" and put their funds into oil wells, race horses, and even a prizefighter! That was not for me. I preferred the N.A.I.C. variety.

At the time I worked more than forty hours a week as public relations director of a major shopping center and belonged to three business organizations. I looked for members for my investment club in the group in which I had been a member the longest. From the club's roster, I picked twenty women whom I liked and who I thought would be interested in joining an investment club, and sent letters inviting them to my home for a preliminary meeting. I quoted parts of the newspaper article which had so impressed me, including the three rules, which, I stated, would be imperative in our club, as well as the condition that we become members of the N.A.I.C. and follow its guidelines.

First Meeting

Twelve people came to my home that first evening, and two others expressed interest, although they were unable to attend. In addition, during the meeting, some of the guests said they knew others to contact. Although I had already sent away for the *Investor's Manual* of the N.A.I.C., it had not yet arrived; so we scheduled another meeting for two weeks later and invited the other interested parties.

Second Meeting

In March we held our second meeting, read aloud from pertinent sections of the *Manual,* agreed to start a club, and began to draw up a partnership agreement fashioned after the one suggested in the *Manual.* I was elected the first president, and we also elected a vice president, a secretary, and a treasurer. You'll note, on reading the *Manual,* that these officers are referred to as the Presiding Partner, Assistant Presiding Partner, Recording Partner, and Financial Partner; but we decided to use the more common (and shorter) terms.

We also decided on the amount of money—$20—to invest each month. I believe most clubs being formed in the eighties are investing $25 to $50—the larger amount is a result of inflation—but we don't find our own sum limiting, as members can contribute in multiples of $20 at any time without unduly disrupting the bookkeeping records.

Some clubs impose an "initiation fee" at the outset which can be used for start-up expenses, such as the N.A.I.C. membership fee and the purchase of manuals and other supplies. Some clubs impose a rather large fee, $100 or more. This practice not only gives the club a good start with its investing program but also serves to ensure that members are serious about their commitment.

Most clubs use the N.A.I.C. bookkeeping method which permits new members to join without having to invest a large sum in order to equal the investment of older members. The recommended system allows members to buy "units" with their monthly contribution, and new members buy as many units as their $20 permits. The value of units is determined monthly by the treasurer, who divides the total value of the club by the units already in existence.

Meeting Place

We next discussed a permanent meeting place. Fortunately, one of our members worked in a law firm and volunteered the use of its conference room. When this person resigned from the club years later, we met in each other's homes until we found a community room at a local savings and loan company.

Other clubs have used similar facilities; one that I know of meets at the local country club and another at a university. One club, which has a doctor as a member, uses a room at a medical clinic after hours, and still another meets at its broker's office. The latter is risky in my opinion, as there are dangers to having a broker too closely involved in the workings of the club, which I'll discuss in more detail later.

We had members suggest names for the club, choosing the one that received the most votes, and then decided on a regular date— the first Tuesday of each month—for our meetings.

One club I visited, which meets in members' homes, gets together on Friday evenings at 7:30 and then takes a break to turn on the television set and watch "Wall Street Week," the PBS stock market program.

Most clubs meet in the evenings, but occasionally one will meet during the day, usually after lunch (sometimes the members use the lunch hour as a social period so that their meetings can be strictly business).

Next we selected a broker. I had recently heard of a registered representative in a well-known stock brokerage firm who was familiar with investment clubs, and suggested that he be the club's broker; this met with approval. (Over the years, incidentally, various brokers worked for us, and at the moment we deal with a discount broker.) In addition we voted to join the N.A.I.C. and to purchase manuals for each member.

Third Meeting

By the April meeting, we had a typed partnership agreement and this was read and voted upon; each member then signed it. We planned to limit the club to fifteen members; but two of the original guests asked for more time in which to consider joining, and since we had fourteen signatures, we made our limit sixteen. Then the treasurer collected the first $20 from each person.

MEMBERS

Some further notes on whom to invite into your club may be helpful at this point. As I've already stated, it's vital to have congenial people with approximately the same goals for the club; this may become a long-term commitment. I suggest that any potential new member be a *very good* friend of the person proposing the membership.

Another important consideration is that members must feel committed to taking an active part in the club. We're all familiar with groups in which a handful of members do all the work and everyone else merely shows up and pays dues. In some cases they don't even show up. You don't want members whose attitude is "Here's my money; make me rich!" That's detrimental to an investment club.

Even if members are willing to contribute their $20 to $50 a month and have no voice in investment decisions (to my surprise, there are many of them), it's not fair that the remaining members shoulder all the work of learning how to evaluate stocks and prepare necessary information to determine what and when to buy.

I'm reminded that one of the investment clubs I was asked to visit consisted of members of another type of club. In this club it was the practice to elect a four-member Board of Directors who had the responsibility for enacting all the club's business, and when I attended the second meeting of the investment club I found they intended to operate in the same fashion.

I interrupted their meeting and reminded them that this was a partnership: each person put in the same amount of money (at least initially) and had an equal right and opportunity to say where it should be invested. They revised their plans accordingly and are operating quite successfully now in the suggested manner. (Suggestions for conducting investment club meetings will be found in a later chapter.)

Other places to look for club members are among your business associates, relatives, neighbors, or members of your church committee or union. One group originally consisted of young women whose children attended the same school. Another had been a bowling team. One was a group of senior citizens attending a program at the local recreation center. Still another began with members of an adult singles group at a church.

You needn't find all ten or fifteen members yourself. Simply invite those you would like in your club and ask each of them to choose one or two others who are close to them and would have the same investment goals. Feeling comfortable with everyone in the club can't be stressed too strongly; some clubs have even restricted their membership to nonsmokers (or at least to those who can refrain from smoking during the meetings).

PARTNERSHIP AGREEMENT

The *Investor's Manual* provides a copy of the partnership agreement of The Mutual Investment Club of Detroit, which was formed on February 1, 1940, and is the oldest still-operating investment club known to the N.A.I.C. The partnership agreement reproduced in Appendix A is that of a California club. I suggest that after your own partnership agreement is prepared an attorney look it over to be sure it adheres to your state laws.

The first item in your partnership agreement should be the name of your club; then the date on which you begin operations; third, the purpose.

It's here that some clubs limit themselves to common stocks. Others allow anything that isn't specifically prohibited, such as buying on margin or selling short. (These terms will be explained in detail later.) Some clubs buy warrants, some buy preferred stocks, and one club I visited bought gold. Performance records seem to indicate, however, that clubs which stick strictly to buying common stocks do best in the long run.

Club Meetings

Meetings are listed in the partnership agreement and generally consist of general meetings, usually held monthly. In the agreement specify the meeting date (first Tuesday of the month, for example) and time (7:30 P.M., for example). The date of the annual meeting for election of officers and special meetings should also be listed. Provision for special meetings is important because there may be times when the president or a group of members feels such a step is necessary. To avoid frivolous calling of special meetings you should provide that at least two members must call it and that the notice must be in writing to all members.

Generally, no notice of meetings is given to members except for the annual meeting, and this should be mailed at least five days in advance. If you provide for it in your partnership agreement, you can also permit telephone notices at least one day before the meeting date. You should also establish how many members of your club will constitute a quorum and what steps you will take if a quorum is not present at the start of a meeting.

Club Officers

Our club has a president, a vice president, a secretary, and a treasurer. We've used these names because they're familiar ones and shorter than the terms Presiding Partner, Assistant Presiding Partner, and so on, given in the partnership agreement found in the N.A.I.C. *Investor's Manual.*

Some clubs don't have a vice president, but someone needs to act in the event of the absence of the president and we think it's helpful to indicate who that person shall be. It's also advance training for the job of president, as the vice president is usually nominated for the office of president the following year.

The vice president can do more than simply wait around; he or she can be put in charge of your stock study program. Whether this is something your club will want to do depends on your members, and additional information about organizing a study program will be found in the next chapter.

The secretary takes minutes of all the meetings and gives notice of annual and special meetings. It's helpful if the secretary types up a list of current addresses and telephone numbers and distributes it to the members. The secretary would handle any correspondence except the treasurer's; generally there is very little, if any, required.

The treasurer's job is the most difficult and time-consuming, including collecting and depositing funds, keeping the books, making a written monthly report to the members, and executing orders for the club whenever the members have voted to buy or sell stock. There are now computer programs that will prepare these reports; if one of your members has a personal computer and is willing to do so, he or she could become permanent treasurer. One gentleman I've heard of augments his retirement income by performing this task for several clubs in his area.

Provide, in your partnership agreement, the method to handle a vacancy among these officers. For a one-meeting absence the president may appoint someone to carry on those duties, but in the case of resignation, death, or the inability of an officer to perform his or her duties you should spell out how the election will be held and whether it will be temporary or not.

Monthly Contributions

It's important to provide the amount of contributions required of each member and also the date at which they must be made. Some clubs impose a fine on a member who fails to make this payment within ten days after the meeting date. This not only is for the convenience of the treasurer, but is important for the future of the club, as a constant amount of money available for investing every month is necessary for the club to prosper.

Rules for how the treasurer lists the value of the partnership should also be a part of the partnership agreement, along with a specific date on which the valuation is to be made. Each member is entitled to a written statement of the value of the club and of his or her personal capital account in the club every month. The *Accountant's Manual* provided by the N.A.I.C. gives detailed instructions for setting up the financial records; I suggest that all clubs send for this and use it, even if they don't join the association.

Safeguards for members should be provided in the agreement; for example, it should state that members manage the club in proportion to the size of their capital accounts. This means that voting to buy or sell stock is not a "one member–one vote" proposition. Each member votes the number of units he or she holds. For example, a long-time member who has 200 units would vote 200 units; another member, who joined recently and has only 20 units can vote only 20 units. The older member's vote, therefore, carries more weight than that of the newer member. This is a fair means of conducting the business of the club, as generally the members with the greatest number of units not only are more experienced and longer-term club members, but have more at stake.

Further protection for all partners should be given by a clause which states that no member may vote more than 20 percent of the club's total value. Such a provision is necessary so that a member who has been in the club for a long time or who has increased his or her contributions can't exert an undue influence over the other members.

Profits and losses of the club are borne by the members in proportion to their capital accounts, so that those who have the largest number of units will, at the end of the year, receive more of the capital appreciation of the club than those who have fewer. This should be spelled out, along with the fact that the books must be available and open to inspection by any partner. Another protection to spell out is that an annual audit by a committee of the members must be made.

If the club maintains a bank account, it should be listed in the partnership agreement. Most clubs do have such accounts, as it's more convenient to deposit the members' checks into it and write one check to the broker to buy stocks or add to the club's money market fund. Two officers of the club should have their names on the bank account and two persons should be required to sign checks.

Broker

In my opinion it's very important to prohibit, in the partnership agreement, a stockbroker from being a member of the club. The most obvious problem you might have with a broker-member is a possible conflict of interest. (Is the broker-member suggesting we sell that stock because he or she really feels it's the right decision, or only because of a desire to make a commission on the sale?)

Further possible disadvantages are that the broker-member will be given too much responsibility, that other members won't feel free to disagree with him, and that members will tend to become lazy and shirk their homework, so that they learn nothing about investing.

Finally, should this member leave one brokerage to go to another, the club may be forced to move its account, perhaps creating some ill will, as well as extra paperwork for the treasurer and other officers.

The partnership agreement should stipulate that a broker account be set up and specify which partner will be the liaison with that broker and the exact method of authorizing buy and sell decisions. An example of a broker's agreement will be found in Appendix B.

Other Provisions

No partner should be compensated for his or her services to the club, although (as you'll see in a later chapter) some clubs give a small gift to their treasurer, who does the lion's share of the paperwork. Reimbursement for expenses, however, is proper and should be indicated.

A limit on your members should be included in the partnership agreement; most clubs limit their membership to between ten and fifteen. Long experience has shown that this number seems to result in the most successful clubs. Having too few members can inhibit investing; having too many can be unwieldy. You should also state whether new members are to be admitted (up to your limit) on a majority or a unanimous vote of the membership. I think a unanimous vote is important, but each club must make this determination for itself.

Provision should be made for termination of the club, indicating how all proceeds will be distributed; in addition, the agreement should provide that members can come and go from time to time without upsetting the routine of the club. The valuation statement of the preceding month is used to determine a withdrawing partner's account, and it must be decided if there will be a penalty attached to this withdrawal. If the club's money is fully invested in stocks and a member wishes to leave, some stocks would have to be sold to accommodate him or her; therefore it's sensible to establish, in advance, what this penalty will be. The N.A.I.C. suggests charging 3 percent of the amount being withdrawn, or the brokerage commissions involved in selling the necessary stock to provide the funds, whichever is higher.

The partnership agreement should also provide that members can withdraw cash without leaving the club so that, if a member has joined in order to save for a child's education, buy a home, or start a business, the member can achieve the investment goal.

A list of "forbidden acts" should be established in the partnership agreement. For example, no member will be given the right or authority to obligate the partnership for anything other than the matter of buying or selling stocks as provided for in the agreement. Members shouldn't be permitted to assign their share in the partnership to anyone else; to do so should result in their immediate ouster from the club. Members shouldn't use the partnership name or credit for any other purpose, and they should do nothing which would make it impossible to carry on the business of the club.

Some clubs forbid members to buy stock on margin, to sell short, or to trade in options or commodities; some even go so far as to limit the price or the price-earnings ratio of stocks to be purchased. Read the suggested partnership agreement in Appendix A or in the *N.A.I.C. Investor's Manual* and discuss these points with your members thoroughly before making them part of your agreement.

Finally, provision must be made for amending the agreement, by majority, two-thirds, or any other designated proportion of the membership. It's usually stipulated that certain paragraphs, such as those having to do with meetings, partnership withdrawal, death of a partner, purchase price for a withdrawing partner, and forbidden acts, cannot be amended except by unanimous and written vote of the members. Members then sign a typed copy of the agreement and are given one to keep. Members who join later are also required to sign and are given a copy of the document.

Sometimes, when a new club is being formed, potential members don't understand the various provisions of the partnership agreement, and may wish to rewrite it or substitute one of their own. It's suggested that they adopt the agreement provided in Appendix A or the one suggested by the N.A.I.C. at the outset, with the proviso that at the end of six months they can make any changes they feel are necessary. It's usually found that the agreement proposed is well-suited to investment clubs and has many built-in protections.

As stated before, it's important to have an attorney go over the agreement so that it protects the club and its members from any unusual liability or taxes. Details on this subject can be found in the N.A.I.C. *Investor's Manual.*

The agreement form between the club and its broker, as mentioned earlier, is found in Appendix B. This isn't lengthy and merely spells out the procedure for investing by the club and protects both the club members and the broker from any misunderstanding. Such a form is suggested by the N.A.I.C. and a sample is given in the *Investor's Manual.*

As I mentioned in an earlier chapter, I strongly recommend that an investment club join the N.A.I.C. Failing that, it should send for the books, forms, and other material provided by them; this will contribute much to the ease of organization and profitable operation of the club.

Operating the Club

6

RULES

Now that your club is formed, let's discuss its operations. If your partnership agreement follows the one suggested in this book, many of these details have already been decided.

If on the other hand your partnership agreement, like the one found in the N.A.I.C. *Investor's Manual,* covers only the broad aspects of club organization goals and membership, many details remain to be considered. In that case, draw up a list of rules or operating procedures.

First, the duties of the club officers and the procedures for electing the officers should be spelled out in detail.

Next determine the dates and time of your meetings, including the annual meeting date, usually the anniversary of the meeting at which you elected your first officers. Specify handling of special meetings.

Third, set the amount of your monthly contribution and make arrangements for making additional contributions, should members desire to do this. Some club members increase their share of units by buying more during bear markets, when prices dip. For example, they contribute $40 instead of $20 for several months in a row. This is a form of dollar-cost averaging, which, as you'll see later, is an advantage.

Some clubs establish a rule imposing a fine on a member who fails to make the monthly contribution on time. One very successful club in the Midwest also imposes fines for missing a meeting or failing to do a stock study when assigned. Not only do these fines keep the members on their toes, but the occasional extra money increases their investment capital.

The club members should also establish rules for permitting guests and prospective members to attend meetings, and procedures for admitting new members.

Next, determine how the treasurer will report to the members and maintain records. It's probably a good idea to establish in writing that the treasurer is to follow the accounting procedures outlined in the *Accounting Manual* obtained from the N.A.I.C.

Briefly, these procedures include the following four types of records:

1. Cash received and spent.
2. Stocks purchased and sold, and their cost and dividends, if any.
3. Members' record sheets, showing contributions and the number of valuation units owned.
4. Monthly statement of club's position.

The first two are simple and self-explanatory. The easiest way to keep members' records is to use "valuation units." When a club is begun a member's contribution (assuming equal contributions) buys one unit. Therefore the value of the unit is initially the same as the contribution. As expenses are incurred and the value of the club's stocks changes, this number will also change. For example, if the ten members of a new club each contribute $20, there will be ten valuation units, a total of $200 invested, and each unit will be worth $20.

The equation is: Total Club Value divided by Number of Units equals Value of Unit.

A month later, however, after the purchase of $20 worth of club supplies, the situation may look like this:

$$\$180 \div 10 = \$18.00$$

When a member makes a contribution the second month, he or she buys more than one unit, since one could be bought for $18, but the member is contributing $20. This equation is: Member's

Contribution divided by the Current Value of the Unit equals the Number of Valuation Units $20 will buy, or:

$$\$20 \div \$18.00 = 1.1111$$

Several years later the member's record sheet (Individual Valuation Units Ledger) might look like Table 6-1, and the club's Monthly Valuation Statement might resemble Table 6-2. These may look complicated, but they are arrived at by using the simple formulas just explained.

In many clubs the treasurer has an assistant, who then becomes the treasurer the following year, just as the president has a vice president who will take over. In others the treasurer keeps the job for two years, learning the first year and finding it much easier the second. In still other clubs the treasurer may keep the job far longer, the annual audit preventing any abuses of this trust. Since the treasurer's job is probably the most time-consuming, its rotation may be desirable. However, whether it's

TABLE 6-1 Individual Valuation Units Ledger

Name: John Doe				*Social Security Number:* 000-00-0000	
Date Paid	*Paid This Month*	*Total Paid in to Date*	*Total Paid in to Date Including Earnings Reinvested*	*Valuation Units Purchased This Date*	*Total Valuation Units*
1-01-81	Adjusted Balance**	$2,200	$3,693.43	0.0000	239.4568
1-13-81	$ 20	2,220	3,713.43	0.9030	240.3598
2-10-81	20	2,240	3,733.43	1.0839	241.4437
3-10-81	20	2,260	3,753.43	0.9998	242.4435
4-14-81	20	2,280	3,773.43	0.8732	243.3167
5-12-81	120	2,400	3,893.43	4.9854*	248.3021
6-09-81	20	2,420	3,913.43	0.7502	249.0523
7-14-81	20	2,440	3,933.43	0.8345	249.8868

*6 × 0.8309
**At the end of every year, the earnings and capital gains (or losses) are distributed to the members in relation to the number of units held by each. This distribution is reported on the members' income tax return, and an adjusted balance is shown on the ledger at the start of the next year.

TABLE 6-2 Investment Club Valuation Statement August 11, 1981

Securities	Number of Shares	Cost per Share	Total Cost	Closing, 8-7-81	Total Value
Gibson-Homans	100	$14.43	$ 1,443.27	$13.500	$ 1,350.00
Mary Kay	400	12.40	4,959.77	33.000	13,200.00
Natomas	50	39.73	1,986.38	35.375	1,768.75
Tandy Corporation	400	6.86	2,759.26	33.625	13,450.00
Texaco	100	39.87	3,987.36	36.625	3,662.50
Tiger International	50	22.19	1,109.64	21.125	1,056.25
			$16,245.68		$34,487.50
Cash in bank					26.34
Cash in money market fund					9,962.66
Total club value					44,476.50

Total units this date: 1766.2695

Value of each unit: $44,476.50 ÷ 1766.2695 = $25.1810
Number of units each $20.00 will buy in August: $20.00 ÷ $25.1810 = 0.7942

Cash on hand 7-14-81		$4,646.44
Membership Contributions	$ 300.00	
Sale of Stocks*	6,413.20	
Purchase of Stocks*		$1,443.27
Bank Service Charge		$ 1.07
Money Market Dividend	73.70	
Cash on hand, 8-11-81		$9,989.00

*Names of stocks, number of shares, price, etc., would be spelled out in full on this or another sheet.

rotated or not, some clubs give a small gift, such as paying for the treasurer's dinner at their annual night out, to show their appreciation.

The work of the treasurer is made easier by the use of computer programs already in existence, which are frequently advertised in the pages of *Better Investing*. In addition, the N.A.I.C. offers a year-end accounting program to help in closing the books before the annual audit, and for the members' income tax records. A computer-owning member might become permanent treasurer because of the ease of performing these tasks with pre-programmed software. If club bookkeeping is done on a computer, the treasurer should be reimbursed for legitimate expenses incurred, such as floppy disks or computer time.

The foregoing is not meant to discourage readers; most treasurers comment that the N.A.I.C. *Accounting Manual* is so clear that it's not difficult to keep these records, and many even enjoy the few hours they spend at it.

When setting down the club rules, identify the person—usually the treasurer—who will be the contact person between the club and its broker and the N.A.I.C. Decide whether you want your stock certificates in your own safety deposit box at a bank or left in street name with your broker.

The N.A.I.C. suggests that the club keep its own certificates, and I recommend it as well. Should anything happen to the brokerage house, you would not have to wait until its problems were untangled before selling your securities when you wish. Since investment clubs are rarely in-and-out traders (two to five years is the usual length of time a club holds a stock), it's not often the club treasurer has to go to the bank, remove the certificates, and surrender them to the broker.

Finally, set up a meeting agenda, which will be followed regularly, such as:

1. Call to order
2. Minutes of previous meeting
3. Treasurer's report
4. Stock watcher's report (if you have one) or reports by members on the club's stocks that they follow.
5. Vice president's report on investment program
6. Old business
7. New business
8. Adjournment

As you know by now, most clubs have four officers; president, vice president, secretary, and treasurer. The *Investor's Manual* mentions another "specialist" in the club, a "club economist," who may or may not take the place of the "stock watcher." Read this section of the *Manual* to determine if your club has someone who could qualify and if the club could profit from this idea.

In our club we have a stock watcher as a fifth officer. This person keeps track of all our stocks, using large charts to show the price changes and keeping up-to-date Portfolio Management Guides (available through the N.A.I.C.) on each. She reports at each meeting and announces the rate of earnings gain (or loss) each quarter as reported by those companies.

As it happens, this person is also interested in market timing and follows six (at one time it was fourteen) different stock market indicators which give a broad picture of when the market as a whole is in a "bull" or "bear" phase. She began this study during 1973, and it accurately predicted the end of the bear market in December 1974.

There is a further advantage, we feel, to having a stock watcher. The N.A.I.C. suggests, and many clubs follow, the practice of "assigning" club stocks to different members to keep track of and to report on at each meeting. This sounds an ideal method of maintaining members' interest, as well as handling this duty; but in our experience members must occasionally be absent for legitimate reasons and consequently no report is made, or the member has not done the required "homework" before the meeting and so is unprepared.

Another point to consider is that you may have fifteen members and only four stocks. Who gets the honor (or chore?) of watching and reporting on them? You may have ten members and twelve stocks; which members must do twice as much work? If the task is left to the member who first proposed the stock, there may be another problem, as it's common for some members to propose many stocks, whereas others propose few, if any.

The club stock watcher, on the other hand, will report regularly on all stocks. If unable to attend a meeting, the stock watcher can turn over the report to the president or another member to present at the meeting. A further advantage is that not having proposed all the stocks, he or she can report objectively on them.

Although the involvement of all members is desirable, it might be wise, at least in the beginning, to give only one person this responsibility. The office can rotate through the membership, or one person can do it for several years, as long as all the members are willing. Later, when you're sure all your members are conscientious about keeping track of stocks, you can delegate the work to the others.

BROKER

If you haven't chosen a broker yet, do it immediately. If no one in the club knows such a person, you can find one by contacting brokerage houses in your area and asking if they have a registered representative who is familiar with investment clubs. (This step is not necessary when dealing with a discount broker.)

When an interested broker is selected, invite him or her to a meeting and discuss what you both expect for a successful and comfortable relationship (not applicable for discount brokers). Have prepared, and present to the broker, a broker agreement, such as the one in Appendix B.

The broker agreement should contain the name of the broker and the name of your club and authorize the broker to honor the buy and sell orders from your treasurer, who should be specified by name and whose signature should appear on the document.

The agreement should state that the club assumes all responsibility for orders placed by the treasurer or any other member of the club and protects the broker from responsibility for any losses as a result of those orders.

The authorization is binding on the members of the club and their estates and continues until cancelled by a written notice to the broker, except that the broker will also be authorized to make any transactions ordered before receipt of the written notice. Further, the present brokerage firm, and any successor firm, is also protected from liability by the agreement.

The broker's agreement should then be dated, signed by the present club officers and then signed, as witnesses, by all other members.

This agreement should be updated yearly or whenever: the contact person changes, members withdraw from the club, or new members join. This requirement is not as rigorous as it would seem; most clubs retain the same person as treasurer for at least two years, and, with a limit on the number of members allowed, often have no changes in membership for many years. To be sure the agreement is up to date, however, it should be checked once a year, when new officers take over.

Thereafter your broker should not be expected—or invited—to attend your meetings more than once a year. At first glance it would seem that if your broker is willing to attend every meeting, it would be a good idea; however, I'm familiar with clubs which have the broker attend every meeting and their results are no better (and in some cases are worse) than the results of those clubs that rarely see their broker, or those that use a discount broker.

One member of a local club confided to me that having the broker there was very detrimental in the club's early years and they changed brokers to alleviate this problem. In another club, I was told, "In our experience, the less advice you get from the broker, the better."

As discussed in Chapter 2, a broker can have many reasons to recommend a stock to a club other than that it's the best stock for that club at that time. Even when the motive behind the suggestion is absolutely pure, it's possible that the quality of research done by the brokerage is not as good as that of the club members themselves.

The members follow fewer stocks and can study each one more thoroughly than a broker, who must keep track of hundreds of stocks for many clients. More important, your broker-client relationship will be more pleasant if you don't take up too much of the broker's valuable time.

Perhaps the most important consideration in respect to the growth of the club is that having a broker in attendance regularly is similar to having a broker-member, with the same disadvantages: the members will rely too heavily on the broker's advice, hesitate to disagree with him or her, and not spend enough of their own time learning how to evaluate stocks. An investment club is a learning experience, and anything which detracts from this will retard club growth and profitability.

In clubs using full-service brokers, the procedure for most of the year is for the contact person to call the broker prior to the meeting to ask if there is any information regarding stocks the club owns or any suggestions for new stocks; of course the contact will phone the broker as soon as possible after the meeting if there are any buy or sell orders.

Such brokers can provide materials about stocks for your members to peruse. These may be Standard & Poor's stock reports or they may be reports prepared by the research department of that particular brokerage. Don't make it a habit, however, to ask for a large number of these. Two or three per month will be more than adequate for club needs, at least in the early years, and will not strain the broker-client relationship.

Never call your broker merely to check the price of stocks you own or are considering. You can look this up in the newspaper. If your treasurer, or any other member, has a computer and one of the database services, price quotes are available for a small fee, which should, of course, be reimbursed.

Don't be tardy in paying for stocks purchased, or in surrendering stock certificates when selling. Five working days is usually the deadline, and your broker—as well as your club—will suffer if you don't meet it.

DISCOUNT BROKERS

In the early years of your club, it may be a good idea to use a full-service broker. The help in the form of reports and up-to-date information that you get may be well worth the additional commissions you pay.

However, if you find that you rarely follow your broker's advice, if you find it easier to go to the library for information, or if your broker doesn't give you sufficient information about stocks you hold, it may be time to consider switching to a discount broker.

Although fees may vary among different houses and there are minimum charges, a discount broker can save you as much as 76 percent in commission charges. For example, on a 100-share order of a $55 stock, a full-service broker might charge $92 in commissions, whereas the discount broker would charge $45, a saving of 51 percent.

One well-known discount broker charges a minimum of $18 plus 1.2 percent of the principal amount on orders of $3,000 or less. This means that if your club invests $1,000, the commission would be $30, or 3 percent. A full-service broker might charge as much as 6 percent for this same transaction.

Another advantage often available from discount brokers is a twenty-four-hour telephone number you can use for quotes and for placing orders.

The disadvantages are that you must spend more time seeking stock market information so that you keep abreast of developments in the companies in which you own stock, and that you must find your own potential investments and the information you need about them. Once again, a computer can come to your aid, as you can check regularly for late news about your portfolio stocks.

MEETINGS

Most investment clubs meet in the evening; 7:30 to 9:30 P.M. is a popular time. The president should see that the meetings proceed smoothly and efficiently, with a minimum of social chatter, as experience has proved that those clubs which operate in a businesslike manner usually continue longer and are the most successful. I know of a club which meets only sporadically and then complains because so few members attend!

During the first year of operation, a club's many start-up and learning activities should keep its members interested and busy. A study program during the first year should begin with the *Manual*. After officers are elected, and club guidelines are drawn up, at each of the next four meetings one member can read aloud a section of the *Manual* and it can be discussed, so that each person understands it. The N.A.I.C. has a correspondence course, which might also be helpful at this point.

Thereafter, the bulk of meetings are concerned with the investment program your club wishes to follow, or discussing which stocks to buy or evaluating those you already own.

While the club is young, an educational program is useful. The president or vice president can assign lectures or "lessons" on various aspects of the financial scene, such as:

1. Learning the various terms used. A glossary is included in this book as well as in the N.A.I.C. *Manual*.
2. Study of fundamental analysis of stocks, including understanding annual reports with their balance sheets and income statements.
3. Reporting on new (or classic) stock market books that might give insight to the members.
4. Investigation of new or different investment theories.

In addition to study of the market as a whole and your stocks (owned or proposed) in particular, there are many ways of maintaining members' interest in the club.

From time to time, especially when new members are admitted, the club can give lessons on preparing the Stock Selection Guide. A blown-up version of this Guide on heavy cardboard is available from the N.A.I.C. and one person can explain and fill in this large chart, while individual members follow along with their own regular-size Stock Selection Guides.

One or more members might attend an N.A.I.C. Council meeting in your area and give an in-depth report on what took place. Councils frequently have speakers who are stock brokers, advisors, public relations directors of corporations in the area, and so on. Usually the meetings are free. A member might attend and report on the National Investors Congress. Dates and places of both Council and Congress meetings are well-publicized in *Better Investing*.

A member from a successful older club in your area could be invited to speak and answer questions by your members.

If companies in which you've purchased stock, or propose to do so, are located in your area, you might ask their public relations departments if someone would like to speak at your meeting, or you might be able to arrange a tour through their facilities. A member might attend the annual stockholders' meeting of a company in which you own stock, and report on it.

If the club uses a full-service broker, this person can attend one meeting a year and present ideas or answer questions. This meeting might even be held in the brokerage office, where its workings could be explained to you.

Social events can be planned from time to time, such as a dinner meeting at a local restaurant. Our club holds its December meeting in a restaurant and invites past members to join us that evening if they wish.

One all-women club has a special meeting once a year to which they invite their husbands, and the men conduct the meeting. The husband of the president becomes the presiding officer for that meeting, the husband of the Secretary has to read minutes and take notes, etc. The men discuss stocks, and, if they choose to, can even buy something. They're prohibited, however, from selling anything the club already owns! A friendly rivalry exists when comparing the results of stocks recommended by their husbands to their own choices.

All meetings have a certain amount of sociability. Whether members have been friends for years or have just met, they'll want to socialize, at least briefly. Even if meetings are held in an office or other meeting room, simple refreshments can be served.

Some clubs offer refreshments in advance, since there's usually a gathering time of ten to twenty minutes. This lets the early ones socialize until the meeting starts. Other clubs set out food and beverages and let members get up and help themselves from time to time throughout the meeting. Still others wait for adjournment and then have a social period of thirty to forty-five minutes. Experiment and see what suits your members and your method of operation. If you meet in members' homes, the host or hostess may be the person who determines when refreshments will be served.

Providing refreshments is usually the responsibility of each member in turn, generally alphabetically by last name. Even if you meet in a community room, this can be planned in advance, with the president announcing, just before adjournment, the date of the next meeting and who will host it.

If you meet during the day a luncheon at a restaurant could precede the meeting. Some restaurants allow groups which have lunch there to use a private room, or a portion of one, to hold meetings, since there's usually a lull in business between lunch and dinner service. Two further advantages of this are that you always have the same meeting place and that you have tables on which to spread out papers and do any writing that may be required.

Another means of sparking interest in your club may be to hold a contest. Many clubs, including ours, have done this over the years. The contest might be one in which members choose—on paper—a stock they think will appreciate the most in value, by percentage, over the next six months (or whatever time period is chosen). The winner can be given a free dinner at your annual dinner-out meeting, if you have one, or some other prize.

Financial services such as Value Line, and newspapers such as *Barron's*, sometimes conduct contests that your members, or the club as a whole, might enter. Or you might arrange a contest between yours and another club in your area.

One all-women club has an ongoing contest ending at its annual meeting each year. The winner gets to drink her mint juleps from a silver trophy cup on which her name is engraved. She then gets to keep the cup until the next annual meeting, when someone else may win.

Each month, as your contest progresses, the members compare their current standings, and often these change dramatically right up to final results.

Besides being fun, such a contest can lead to finding some worthwhile stocks. In our club the stock of Mary Kay Cosmetics won a contest, and afterward the club bought the stock at $48.75. Before a month was out, the stock had split two for one, giving us 200 shares, and a year later split again, giving us 400, which we sold at $26 approximately a year and a half after our purchase, for a profit of 113 percent.

On the other hand, MCI Communications, which was a contest-winning stock a few years later, seemed too high-priced for us by the end of the contest period and we didn't buy it. Its price fell shortly thereafter, which reinforced our belief that sound investigation is necessary before buying any stock.

I hope the following chapters will help you do just that.

Going It Alone 7

The N.A.I.C. allows individual as well as club membership, and in my opinion the best way to learn about the stock market and to invest for the future is to take advantage of the many aids and services of N.A.I.C. membership. Dues are $30 per year and this includes your annual subscription to *Better Investing* magazine.

Most of the material presented in the rest of this book can be of value to individual investors as well as to clubs, but there are some disadvantages to investing alone.

First, solitary investing means isolation. In a club, you not only have social intercourse, but can take advantage of others' opinions and ideas. Ten to fifteen people looking for good stocks to buy find more than one person can. They have more time, collectively, for stock studies. You can bounce ideas off them, ask them questions, pick their brains.

Conservative people may tend to accumulate too "safe" a portfolio, without fellow club members to suggest other types of stocks. Contrariwise, those leaning toward speculative stocks have no one to pull them up short and suggest a less aggressive stance to improve total performance. As we will see, the club as a whole is less likely to become "married" to a stock and afraid to sell it when the right time arrives.

The club also requires discipline. Alone, you may put off

your stock studies this month, but if your club is counting on you, you have an incentive to do it on time. You might try to skimp on your investigations and buy a stock on a whim or tip; but if your club insists you bring a completed Stock Selection Guide to the meeting, you have no choice but to accomplish the necessary homework.

Obviously, more people in the endeavor means more money to invest; more money to invest means lower brokerage commissions. Finally, members of investment clubs may use their accounts for Individual Retirement Accounts (I.R.A.); individual investors must use their brokers for a stock-oriented I.R.A., which will probably cost more.

Most people are social creatures. A few, however, may not have been able to join a club already in existence or may be "loners," and prefer to make their own decisions. Unless you're happy going it alone, I strongly urge you to start your own investment club (see Chapter 5). If you can't get ten members, start with five, and urge each of them to look seriously for friends or relatives as additional members.

RESOURCES FOR THE INDIVIDUAL INVESTOR

American Association of Individual Investors

If you decide not to join or start an investment club, there's another organization which may help. It's the American Association of Individual Investors, 612 North Michigan Avenue, Chicago, Illinois, 60611, formed in 1979 and now consisting of 90,000 members. Present dues are $44 per year and benefits include a ten-issues-per-year *Journal* with articles of interest to investors, an annual book on no-load mutual funds, a year-end tax strategy guide, membership in local chapters, and reduced costs for investment seminars, books, and study programs.

If you're very self-motivated, this may be all you need for successful investing. One man in Illinois, who had at one time been in an investment club, is now a member of this association and gets tax information and general help from its *Journal*. As a business-man, he has contacts with many other companies and knows their management; so his policy is to buy stock in those companies with which he does business.

He holds between eight and twelve different stocks in at least five or six different industries and uses stop loss orders, which will be explained in Chapter 12. One of his successes has been Katy

Industries, which he purchased at $4.50 per share in 1976 and sold at $34.00 per share in 1985, for a profit of 658 percent!

Quaker Oats stock, which he bought early in 1984 at $61.25, has split two for one and is now at $48.50, but he has not taken his 58 percent profit. He continues to hold the stock, along with Waste Management Company and Browning Ferris, which are both in the waste disposal industry.

N.A.I.C. Low Cost Investment Program

If membership in any organization is not your cup of tea, you should know that the N.A.I.C. has a low-cost investment plan enabling individuals to invest small amounts. This program is based on the dividend reinvestment plans offered by some corporations. The N.A.I.C. invested in these plans, and members of the Association can take advantage of this fact to buy small numbers of shares (a minimum of one share to begin) and contribute additional amounts on a regular basis.

When the requirements for that particular corporate plan are met, the stock is then transferred into the name of the owner (you) and from then on you deal directly with the corporation. If you're interested, write to the N.A.I.C. for more details.

A possible drawback is that, since it's not necessary to invest regularly every month or even every quarter, you may allow your payments to drop off, thus aborting the attempt to pursue a meaningful savings plan.

A further drawback may be in the limited number of companies that offer this method of investing. *Better Investing* publishes a list of these corporations; but, although new names are added from time to time, out of the thousands of publicly owned companies, there are only twenty-six available in this plan at this writing. If none of these appeals to you, the program may not suit you. The twenty-six companies presently in the plan are:

Aetna Life and Casualty	Dana Corporation
American Family Corporation	Dayco Corporation
Armco, Inc.	Detroit Edison
Ashland Oil	Walt Disney
Brown–Forman	Dow Chemical Company
Cent. Maine Power Company	Federal–Mogul
Chesebrough–Pond's	Foxboro Company

Gerber Products	McDonald's Corporation
Gould, Inc.	NBD Bancorp
W. R. Grace	Primark Corporation
Harsco	Quaker Oats
Int'l Bank of America	Quanex
Kellogg Company	St. Paul Companies

An investment club I know of, which began in 1983, met with failure because the members did not want to fill out the Stock Selection Guide or do the other work required to keep a club going. So one woman member turned to the Low Cost Plan instead and is doing quite well on her own.

She attended an Investors' Fair in San Francisco and also attended some meetings of the San Francisco Council of the N.A.I.C. At one of these events she heard a speaker from the Quaker Oats Company and was so impressed she bought their stock; like the Illinois man, she has seen it rise and split and rise again. She now owns four more stocks on the Low Cost Plan list.

Sharebuilder

The well-known brokerage firm of Merrill, Lynch, Pierce, Fenner & Smith offers to individuals a low-cost investment plan called Sharebuilder. It allows you to invest as little as $25 and buy fractional shares of almost any company you choose; all those listed on the New York Stock Exchange, all on the American Stock Exchange, and about a thousand over-the-counter stocks.

You must make your own decisions as to what to buy, but suggestions will be sent you from time to time. Reduced brokers' commissions are another benefit. For more information, contact any Merrill, Lynch office or phone 800-221-1856.

As I've said, individuals as well as clubs can join the N.A.I.C., use their Stock Selection Guides and other tools, including *Better Investing,* sign up for their advisory service, attend local council meetings, and write for advice. Or, an individual can merely subscribe to *Better Investing* magazine for $15 a year.

If you wish to go it completely alone, you can still invest successfully in the stock market. All it requires is some discipline and a little work. Determine at the outset how much time you're willing to devote to your investment goals and stick to it. You can't win the game if you don't pay attention.

SETTING GOALS

"To make a lot of money" is not a sensible goal for either an individual or an investment club. The N.A.I.C. suggests clubs aim for long-term appreciation of their portfolios, and that a doubling of value in five years' time is a reasonable, achievable goal. Even if you're not a member of a club, even if you don't belong to the N.A.I.C., you'd be well advised to look in this direction.

Further, the N.A.I.C. suggests that their three main guidelines will enable you to accomplish it. I've mentioned them before, but here are the three rules again, so that you can study them one at a time in greater detail.

1. Invest regularly.
2. Reinvest all dividends.
3. Invest in growth companies.

INVEST REGULARLY

As we will see in Chapter 10, there can be logical reasons why stocks should not be purchased every month, year in and year out. However, the N.A.I.C. argues that if you do buy every month, you will be "dollar-cost averaging"—buying fewer shares when prices are high and more when they're low—and in the long run achieving a better total price for your shares.

For example, if you were to buy 10 shares of a stock every month for a year, and its price varied from a high of $60 to a low of $10, you would be able to buy 120 shares and would spend $4,200, as illustrated in Table 7-1.

In the same example, if you invested approximately the same dollar amount in the stock every month, say, $300 to $350, you would have spent only $3,980, $220 less, but you would have bought 166 shares of the stock, 46 more. Whereas the average cost per share when you bought a fixed *number* per month was $35.00, the average cost when you spent a (relatively) fixed *sum* was $23.97, quite a difference. This works, by the way, whether the stock goes down first and then up, or up first and then down.

Of course in this example your stock is unrealistically volatile, but the principle is the same. Some stocks, however, go down and never come back up. Should the worst happen, and the stock become worthless, the person who bought ten shares per month,

TABLE 7-1 Example of Dollar-Cost Averaging

Same Number of Shares per Month				Same Dollar Amount per Month*			
Month	Price	Number of Shares	Cost	Month	Price	Number of Shares	Cost
Jan.	$60	10	$ 600	Jan.	$60	5	$ 300
Feb.	50	10	500	Feb.	50	7	350
Mar.	40	10	400	Mar.	40	8	320
Apr.	30	10	300	Apr.	30	11	330
May	20	10	200	May	20	17	340
June	10	10	100	June	10	35	350
Jul.	10	10	100	Jul.	10	35	350
Aug.	20	10	200	Aug.	20	17	340
Sep.	30	10	300	Sep.	30	11	330
Oct.	40	10	400	Oct.	40	8	320
Nov.	50	10	500	Nov.	50	7	350
Dec.	60	10	600	Dec.	60	5	300
Totals		120	$4,200	Totals		166	$3,980
Cost per share			$35.00				$23.97

*Since you can't buy less than a full share of stock, some months the amount spent does not equal $350. You would still purchase 166 shares, 46 more than by purchasing a fixed number per month, and have saved $220.

starting at $60, would have lost $2,000 in six months and the one who spent an equal amount every month would have lost slightly more, $2,100.

Buying when a stock's price is falling is called "averaging down." You'd better be very sure the price will come up again some day soon. What you want to avoid is buying more of a stock simply *because* the price is lower. If the stock's price decline is due to earnings decline, or a lower price/earnings ratio, you should sell your stock rather than take the chance it will go down further.

This is well illustrated by an example from my own club. We bought eight shares of Avon Products at $111 each during our second year. The price of the stock dropped as low as $19 during that bear market, and never recovered very much during the strong bull market that began in January 1975.

We bought an additional twelve shares when it recovered to $41, lowering our per-share cost to $69. The stock remained in a trading range of $40 to $50 for a long time, and reached a high of $61 in 1977. The stock's price drifted lower for another year; and we sold our shares near the end of 1978 for $54, for a loss of about

$300, having held them more than six years. If we still held stock today, it would be worth about $22 a share.

Considered one of the top growth companies in the sixties and early seventies, Avon had been as high as $140 per share; therefore $111 seemed a reasonable price in 1973; however, we failed to take into account that price-earnings ratios were unrealistically high in the late sixties and were bound to collapse sooner or later. If we had averaged down when the price was $19, instead of waiting until it was $41, we'd have achieved much better results during the next bull market. With more research we might also have learned that Avon was having difficulty hiring salespeople for door-to-door sales and that, with more and more women entering the work force, there were fewer women at home to purchase cosmetics that way.

As useful as dollar cost averaging is, you need to be very sure you've bought a good company at a reasonable price based upon its own past history, the performance of other stocks in that industry, and the direction of the market as a whole.

It's entirely possible that when using the Stock Selection Guide or any other analysis, you may reach a time when *no* stocks that you've studied seem to be reasonably priced. Should you buy something anyway, choosing the lesser of several evils? When interest rates are high, and money market funds offer 18 percent on your idle funds, should you settle for a 2 percent yield and a possible (not guaranteed) growth rate of 8 percent in a stock?

I don't advocate trying to second-guess the market by in-and-out trading, which can be more speculative than investment-oriented. But the N.A.I.C.'s rule notwithstanding, there will be times over the years when it becomes obvious even to a neophyte that things are not normal and that a cash position makes more sense. There will be more on this subject in a later chapter.

There is another reason my investment club "bent" the N.A.I.C.'s rule, however. From the very beginning, we felt it wasn't practical for a new club. In 1972 the industry had not yet been deregulated. Brokers charged a minimum fee and standard rates for stock transactions. (Even today discount brokers, as well as full-service brokers, continue to make a minimum charge, as mentioned earlier.)

It doesn't take a mathematical genius to figure out that if you invest $300 each month, even a discount broker's fee of $18 plus 1.2 percent of the amount of the transaction will mean a commission charge of $21.60, or 7.2 percent of your investment. (And Some full-service brokers charge a minimum fee of $25 to $35.) Since selling the stock will entail another commission, it becomes plain that your stock has to rise 14 to 23 percent just for you to break even!

Of course, you hope your stock will rise in value—100 percent in five years may be your goal—and then not only will the selling commission percentage drop, but it will be relatively small compared with the 100 percent appreciation. Still, why spend 7 to 10 percent per transaction when, by waiting one month, you can bring it down to 4 or 5 percent? By spending $600 at one time instead $300 twice, you can reduce the discount broker's commission to 4.2 percent.

Therefore, our club decided not to buy stock every month, but every *other* month, a minor change which saved us a lot of money. Why, we reasoned, search hard for a stock whose dividend was 2 to 4 percent higher, when we were wasting that much on commissions?

In the months when we did not buy anything, we continued to study and discuss possible stock purchases and had time for additional research if necessary, while waiting until we had a sizable investment. Those "odd" months also were opportunities for our special activities; our Christmas dinner meeting, a visit to or from our broker, talks by members of other investment clubs or by corporation executives, book reports, and so on. The time certainly wasn't wasted.

As an individual investor, unless you're in the Low Cost or Sharebuilders plan, you may be faced with the same need to make a large enough purchase to keep commission percentages low.

REINVEST ALL DIVIDENDS

This second rule, although followed by most investment clubs, is sometimes ignored by individual investors. Yet, it's very important. Following this rule can significantly improve your investment performance.

We tend to think of capital appreciation of our stock first. If we bought it at $10 per share, we want to be sure it's selling for $20 per share five years from now, and we watch the price fluctuation diligently.

But it's easy to forget the dividends—and the yield they provide—on that stock, which alone can add immeasurably to a satisfactory retirement supplement.

For example, if you were to invest $200 a month, beginning at age forty, and if the yield on your stocks was a mere 4 percent per year, by age sixty you would have over $73,000. If you then began to withdraw the money at the rate of $400 per month, you would still have over $12,000 left at age eighty.

Of course, investment club members usually contribute only about a tenth of the monthly amount in that example. Still, after contributing only $4,800 during those twenty years, with 4 percent annual yield, you would have $7,300 at sixty and at eighty, after having taken out $40 a month for twenty years, you would still have over $1,200 left.

Four percent is low compared with interest rates during inflationary times. Yield on some stocks has been as high as 9 or 10 percent. Cash left in your broker's money market fund between investments may earn more. During the late seventies and early eighties, these funds paid as high as 16 to 18 percent. (See Table 7-2 for compound interest tables.)

Thus you see that dividends alone can increase your investment results by as much as 10 percent or more.

Dividends are important for another reason. Many investors, particularly those at or near retirement, require them for income, and stocks with high yields are therefore highly regarded and unlikely to drop drastically in price during recessions.

A final point, however. Don't refuse to buy a stock because it has low or no dividends, if it's a fine growth company otherwise. While you may look for a 4 percent dividend yield on your investments, don't lose sight of the fact that you need your stocks to appreciate at a much higher rate. Growth must be the prime consideration.

TABLE 7-2 Ten-Year Compound Interest Tables — Based on $1,000*

Year	\multicolumn{6}{c}{Interest Rate}
	4%	7%	10%	12%	15%	20%
1	$1,040	$1,070	$1,100	$1,120	$1,150	$1,200
2	1,082	1,145	1,210	1,254	1,323	1,440
3	1,125	1,225	1,331	1,405	1,521	1,728
4	1,170	1,311	1,464	1,574	1,749	2,074
5	1,217	1,403	1,611	1,762	2,011	2,488
6	1,265	1,501	1,772	1,974	2,313	2,986
7	1,316	1,606	1,949	2,211	2,660	3,583
8	1,369	1,718	2,144	2,476	3,059	4,300
9	1,423	1,838	2,358	2,773	3,518	5,160
10	1,480	1,967	2,594	3,106	4,046	6,192

*Amounts have been rounded off to the nearest dollar.

In regard to taxes, there's no question that capital appreciation is better than dividends. After all, dividends are taxed like regular income, whereas the stock's appreciation is taxed, if held at least six months, as a long-term capital gain, or at about half your usual rate.

INVEST IN GROWTH COMPANIES

This third rule is probably the most important. What constitutes a growth company will be dealt with more specifically in the next chapter, but at this time it should be pointed out that your portfolio should probably be diversified into large and small companies.

Smaller companies mean more risk, but their chances for capital appreciation are also much greater. It's often pointed out that a company making $3 million a year has to earn only $6 million to have doubled its revenues; whereas one earning $100 million must make $200 million to do the same thing. It stands to reason that it's easier to go from 3 to 6 than from 100 to 200.

For your portfolio to double in five years, you need 14.4 percent appreciation every year. Since dividends may earn about 4 percent of that, the companies you choose to invest in should have growth records of between 8 and 12 percent. The larger companies may grow at only 8 percent, but they are stable and less likely to lose value in bear markets; on the other hand, smaller companies could increase rapidly with growth rates of 10 to 12 percent, but could be more vulnerable in bad times.

How do you determine growth rates? Mainly through sales, which will be more thoroughly discussed in the next chapter.

DIVERSIFICATION

A fourth principle suggested by the N.A.I.C. is diversification. It's an application of the truism: "Don't put all your eggs in one basket." If the basket, or your stock, should fail, you'll have lost everything. The other side of the coin is that that one stock might be the one which soars to the stratosphere and makes you a millionaire.

So, compromises are in order. Since none of us knows in advance exactly what will happen to the fortunes of the stocks we pick, it's prudent to spread our risk among several companies, and even several industries. A popular guideline, the "rule of five," states that of five choices, one will do very well, three will be average, and one will do very poorly. Therefore, having at least five stocks will probably not only prevent disasters, but (if one performs really well), will enable you to achieve your goal.

Like everything else, diversification should not be carried to extremes. If you own too many stocks, you'll have merely "average" results, not the 8 to 12 percent appreciation you're looking for. In the early days of your club or personal investment strategy, you'll naturally have a smaller portfolio, but even clubs worth $100,000 probably need no more than ten to twelve different issues. One of the top clubs of 1982, which has a portfolio worth $146,000, confines itself to only six stocks!

Remember you must watch each stock carefully and this takes time. If each club member is responsible for watching one stock, you might be well advised to limit your portfolio to the number of members. If you're doing it alone, it's even more important to have fewer stocks so that you can keep close tabs on them.

OTHER RULES

Some clubs set rules for investing beyond these four suggested by the N.A.I.C. Individuals, too, may set guidelines for themselves. For example, some limit their purchases to stocks selling at less than a predetermined price, such as $40 per share. Others set guidelines on when to sell. (See Chapter 12 on selling.) A few clubs require that a stock have a minimum yield, such as 4 percent. Others establish a maximum price-earnings ratio, for instance, one of 10 or less. In my opinion, these types of restrictions are best left until you have several years of experience in both bull and bear markets.

Finding the Right Stocks

8

WHERE TO LOOK

Where do you find stocks? They're everywhere. Almost everything we see or use in a day's time is the product of a company whose shares we might purchase, from our shampoo (Proctor & Gamble, perhaps?) to our breakfast cereal (Quaker Oats?) to our clothing (Jonathan Logan?) to our automobile (General Motors?). (Depending on your, or your club members', feelings, you may desire not to own companies which manufacture cigarettes or distill liquor or own gambling casinos, and rule them out in advance.)

As we've already discussed, full-service brokers will suggest stocks to you, and reports on companies that their analysts have studied may be picked up in the brokerage office.

Better Investing, which as a member of the N.A.I.C. you will receive monthly, contains articles on companies to study. The newspaper financial pages and magazines such as *Money, Fortune, Barron's, Forbes, Business Week* and *Time* all mention businesses you might wish to investigate.

Television news and commercials may give you ideas. Friends may comment to you on their stock holdings. Your club vice president or stock program director may have assigned you a list of stocks or an industry to study for the next meeting.

The N.A.I.C. suggests a balanced portfolio; some large corporate giants, some small aggressive companies. In addition to these broad categories, you should think of diversification in terms of industries (see Table 8-1). Avoid a preponderance of utilities or banks or airlines or fast food sellers or computer manufacturers, so that if an entire industry should suffer for any reason, your portfolio won't be devastated. At the same time you may want a sampling of some of these industries when they enjoy public favor.

A "Model Portfolio" is suggested by *Better Investing*, reported quarterly in the magazine, and updated periodically. As of April 1985 the following stocks were in the Model Portfolio list:

Company	Industry
Abbott Laboratories	Hospital products
American Home Products	Drugs
Comair	Airline
Exxon	Petroleum
General Signal	Electronics

TABLE 8-1 Partial List of Industries

Advertising	Electrical equipment	Packaging
Agricultural Equipment	Electronics	Paper
Airlines	Financial services	Petroleum
Aluminum	Food processing	Publishing
Apparel	Gambling casinos	Railroads
Automobiles	Grocery stores	Real estate
Auto parts	Home appliances	Recreation
Banks	Home furnishings	Restaurants
Brewers	Hotels	Retail stores
Broadcasting	Household products	Savings and Loan
Building	Insurance	Securities brokers
Building supplies	Iron	Shoes
Cement	Machinery	Shipping
Chemicals	Machine tools	Soft drinks
Coal	Medical services	Steel
Computers	Medical supplies	Telecommunications
Computer software	Metals	Textile
Copper	Mining	Tire and rubber
Cosmetics	Natural gas	Tobacco
Distillers	Newspapers	Trucking
Defense	Office equipment	Utilities
Drugs		

W.R. Grace	Chemicals
IBM	Office equipment
Kuhlman	Auto products
Magic Chef	Home appliances
Precision Castparts	Machinery
Sea Containers	Shipping
Sears	Retail store

More than just a list of stocks that the editors think have the potential to double in value in five years, this is a balanced portfolio, with different industries represented.

You or your club may be very conservative in nature and put a larger percentage of your funds in utilities and "blue chips," whereas another investor might be on the leading edge of technology and wish to profit—and hope not to suffer—with every company that springs up in Silicon Valley. Whatever suits club members is right for you, so long as the majority agrees on the position taken. If you're an individual investor you can, of course, make this determination alone. There is no dearth of ideas. The real work comes after you've made your list of stocks to study.

WHAT TO LOOK FOR

Sources of information about a company include its prospectus and annual report, but in my opinion the most helpful are reports prepared by three major stock investment researchers: Moody's Handbook of Common Stocks, Standard & Poor's Stock Reports, and Value Line Investment Survey.

You may subscribe to these reports, but they're rather expensive (the Value Line service, for example, costs $395 per year), and need constant updating. An easier approach is to use the bound copies found in your local library. They don't circulate, being reference material, so you must use them on library premises. Often you must ask for them at the reference desk, so don't assume your library doesn't have them if you don't find them on the shelves.

My experience has been that Moody's report is not quite as complete as the other two; however, if that's all your library carries, you can certainly use it.

My custom is to head for the library at least once a month, taking my list of companies to study and my supplies. These consist of my latest copy of *Barron's* (or you may use a recent stock page from any newspaper), supply of Stock Selection Guides, the

N.A.I.C. *Investor's Manual,* pocket calculator, and colored pencils and pens. I then ask the reference librarian for the Value Line books.

I ask for the Value Line books because there are only two of them (the Standard & Poor's reports take up twelve volumes), and I can carry them to a nearby table to work. Also, the Value Line information for one company is all on one side of an 8½- by 11-inch sheet, making it easy to see all the information I want at a glance. Standard & Poor's information, on the other hand, is on two sides of a smaller (about 6 by 9 inch) sheet of paper. A sample of a Value Line page is seen in Figure 8-1.

I try to put my list of stocks in alphabetical order, so that I can look up each one in the Index and mark opposite the name its Value Line page number. That way, I can find it quickly later.

If I don't find a page on one or more companies in Value Line (no service tracks all the thousands of stocks available), I then go to the Standard and Poor's binders on the business-corner shelves of my library. These books are divided, by color, into reports of stocks traded on the New York Stock Exchange, the American Stock Exchange, and over the counter. Sample Standard & Poor's sheets are shown in Figures 8-2 and 8-3.

If I don't know which exchange a stock is traded on, I may have to look through all three sets of Standard & Poor's binders to find it. I may still come up empty-handed at this point, and must then refer to the seven large brown volumes of Standard & Poor's *Corporation Records.* Probably I will give up, however, and cross the name off my list. My reasoning is that, if the stock is so new or so thinly traded that I can't find a report, I may not be able to get enough information on it to analyze it properly. I prefer following a stock closely.

I frequently glance over the Value Line or Standard & Poor's sheet on a company before entering its page number next to the stock on my list. For example, if I see that the price of the stock is too high (some people and some clubs limit the price per share they'll pay)—this information is boldly printed at the top of the page—I can cross it off my list immediately.

Likewise, if the price/earnings ratio of the company—also at the top of the sheet—is too high, I can reject it at once. The price/earnings (or P/E) ratio, as will be explained more fully later, is the number found by dividing the current price of the stock by its current annual earnings per share; it is a sort of barometer indicating what value investors put on the company's earnings.

Theoretically, these numbers can be anything, but the major-

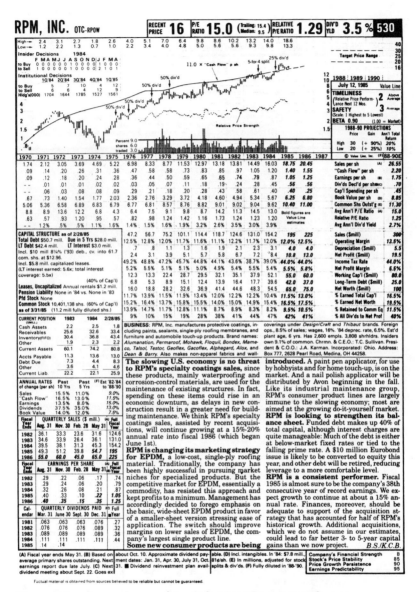

Figure 8-1   A sample page from Value Line Investment Survey.

ity of listed stocks will be found to trade at a P/E ratio between 5 and 30. The thirty stocks which make up the Dow Jones Industrial Average have a current average P/E ratio of 12.2. Some clubs use this as a guideline and don't bother to study any stocks whose ratio

RPM, Inc. 5052

NASDAQ Symbol RPOW   (Incl. in Nat'l Market; marginable)

Price	Range	P-E Ratio	Dividend	Yield	S&P Ranking
May 3'85	1985				
16¾	18⅝-9¾	17	0.56	3.3%	A−

Summary

This manufacturer of specialized chemical protective coatings, and fabrics and wallcoverings, has achieved 37 consecutive years of higher sales and earnings, reflecting internal growth and a successful acquisition program. In its most recent acquisition, the company purchased Westfield Coating Corp., a manufacturer of industrial coatings and inks.

Business Summary

RPM, Inc. manufactures a wide variety of protective coatings (including heavy-duty maintenance, waterproofing, one-part sealants, single-ply roofing, furniture repair and corrosion-controlling coatings) and non-apparel fabrics and wallcoverings (including decorative papers, vinyls and fabrics). Products are marketed in more than 75 countries.

Sales and profits before unallocated expenses for the fiscal year ended May 31, 1984, were derived as follows:

	Sales	Profits
Protective coatings	85%	74%
Fabrics & wallcoverings	15%	26%

Foreign operations accounted for about 4% of sales and 5% of profits in 1983-4.

RPM coating products find applications in exterior surface protection from the effects of moisture and ultra-violet sun rays; corrosion control and rust prevention; furniture repair and restoration; and the hobby, recreational and leisure fields. The company also manufactures and sells four types of single-ply roofing made of plastic or synthetic rubber membrane used as a replacement for conventional hot asphalt roofing. RPM completed its expansion into the single-ply roofing market in 1983-4.

The company markets wallcoverings nationally under the Thibaut trade name, and decorative non-apparel fabrics are sold primarily throughout the Midwest under the Designcraft trade name.

RPM operates 26 manufacturing and distribution facilities throughout North America and one manufacturing facility in Belgium.

The company has been strengthening its industrial and consumer product lines through an active acquisition program (see Important Developments and Finances). Recent acquisitions included Euclid Chemical, Inc., a manufacturer of liquid and powdered additives for the treatment of concrete materials sold to both the restoration and architectural markets (July, 1984), and Testor Corp., a leading manufacturer of hobby paints and accessory items sold nationwide (January, 1984).

Employees: About 1,300.

Important Developments

Jan. '85—The company purchased Westfield Coating Corp. (Westfield, Mass.), a producer of industrial coatings and inks, with sales of about $4 million in 1983.

Next earnings report due in late July.

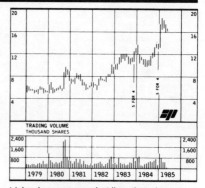

TRADING VOLUME
THOUSAND SHARES

1979 | 1980 | 1981 | 1982 | 1983 | 1984 | 1985

Per Share Data ($)

Yr. End May 31	1984	1983	1982	¹1981	1980	¹1979	¹1978	1977	¹1976	1975
Book Value	4.86	4.72	4.29	3.88	3.42	2.94	2.86	2.51	2.09	1.82
Earnings	³0.87	³0.79	³0.74	³0.66	³0.65	³0.59	³0.50	0.43	0.36	0.27
Dividends	0.40¼	0.34⅝	0.29½	0.24	0.17⅝	0.10⅞	0.07	0.04⅝	0.03	0.02
Payout Ratio	46%	44%	40%	37%	27%	18%	16%	10%	9%	7%
Prices²—High	13¼	10¼	8⅝	9⅞	6½	7	5¼	4	2⅝	1⅞
Low	9¼	5⅝	5⅝	5	4⅞	3⅞	3½	2¼	⅞	⅝
P/E Ratio—	15-11	13-7	12-8	15-8	10-7	12-7	10-7	9-5	7-3	7-3

Data as orig. reptd. Adj. for stk. divs. of 25% Dec. 1984, 25% Nov. 1983, 50% Oct. 1978, 50% Oct. 1977, 50% Oct. 1976, 50% Oct. 1975. 1. Refl. merger or acq. 2. Of preceding cal. yr. 3. Ful. dil.; 0.85 in 1984, 0.78 in 1983, 0.73 in 1982, 0.64 in 1981, 0.63 in 1980, 0.58 in 1979, 0.48 in 1978.

Standard OTC Stock Reports
Vol. 51/No. 55/Sec. 22

May 13, 1985
Copyright © 1985 Standard & Poor's Corp. All Rights Reserved

Standard & Poor's Corp.
25 Broadway, NY, NY 10004

Figure 8-2   Side one of a Standard & Poor's report.

Income Data (Million $)

Year Ended May 31	Oper. Revs.	Oper. Inc.	% Oper. Inc. of Revs.	Cap. Exp.	Depr.	Int. Exp.	Net Bef. Taxes	Eff. Tax Rate	Net Inc.	% Net Inc. of Revs.
1984	154	18.5	12.0%	3.80	3.37	3.18	13.7	38.9%	8.38	5.4%
1983	131	15.3	11.7%	5.49	2.33	2.46	³11.9	38.7%	7.17	5.5%
1982	125	15.2	12.2%	5.22	2.09	2.32	³11.8	43.6%	⁴6.68	5.4%
1981	119	13.2	11.1%	3.85	1.89	1.88	10.7	44.2%	5.81	4.9%
¹1980	114	13.2	11.6%	2.49	1.60	1.89	10.5	44.8%	5.71	4.0%
1979	101	11.8	11.7%	4.59	1.28	1.17	9.8	45.7%	5.14	5.1%
¹1978	75	9.1	12.1%	1.55	1.11	0.90	7.3	47.3%	3.85	5.1%
¹1977	57	7.3	12.8%	1.41	0.84	0.55	6.0	48.7%	3.09	5.5%
1976	47	5.9	12.5%	2.55	0.75	0.56	4.8	49.1%	2.43	5.2%
¹1975	35	4.5	12.8%	0.60	0.58	0.46	3.6	48.3%	1.87	5.3%

Balance Sheet Data (Million $)

May 31	Cash	Assets	Current Liab.	Ratio	Total Assets	Ret. on Assets	Long Term Debt	Common Equity	Total Cap.	% LT Debt of Cap.	Ret. on Equity
1984	2.46	74.2	22.1	3.4	120	7.7%	39.6	54.5	97.1	40.8%	15.8%
1983	2.24	60.1	22.2	2.7	91	8.1%	17.7	48.3	68.0	26.1%	15.4%
1982	5.00	57.0	21.9	2.6	85	8.3%	16.4	44.6	62.1	26.4%	15.5%
1981	3.01	50.4	18.3	2.8	76	7.9%	13.9	41.4	56.1	24.7%	14.7%
1980	2.10	47.7	18.2	2.6	70	8.4%	12.4	36.9	50.3	24.6%	16.3%
1979	2.34	44.3	15.6	2.8	66	8.9%	15.1	32.6	48.6	31.0%	16.7%
1978	3.32	33.1	10.7	3.1	48	8.5%	8.9	28.2	37.1	24.1%	14.9%
1977	3.36	22.6	9.3	2.4	34	9.7%	5.3	18.8	24.1	22.0%	17.7%
1976	2.01	19.0	6.7	2.8	30	9.5%	6.8	16.0	22.8	30.0%	16.4%
1975	1.61	13.8	4.2	3.3	21	8.9%	3.2	13.8	16.9	18.7%	14.5%

Data as orig. reptd. **1.** Refl. merger or acq. **2.** Refl. acctg. change. **3.** Incl. equity in earns. of nonconsol. subs.

Net Sales (Million $)

Quarter:	1984-5	1983-4	1982-3	1981-2
Aug.	49.3	39.6	34.6	36.1
Nov.	¹54.4	38.1	33.9	33.3
Feb.	39.8	31.3	26.4	23.6
May		45.3	36.1	31.5
	154.2	131.0	124.5

Net sales for the nine months ended February 28, 1985 rose 26% from the year-earlier levels, as restated to include Westfield Coating. A 31% increae in selling, general and administrative expenses restricted operating margins, and pretax income was up 24%. After taxes at 43.0%, versus 42.9%, and minority interest, net income advanced 23%, to $8,373,413 ($0.80 a share), from $6,835,058 ($0.66, as adjusted for the November, 1984, 5-for-4 stock split).

Common Share Earnings ($)

Quarter:	1984-5	1983-4	1982-3	1981-2
Aug.	0.40	0.32	0.29	0.29
Nov.	¹0.30	0.26	0.24	0.22
Feb.	0.10	0.08	0.06	0.05
May		0.21	0.20	0.18
	0.87	0.79	0.74

1. Incl. Westfield Coatings Corp. for six months.

Dividend Data

Cash has been paid each year since 1969. A dividend reinvestment plan is available.

Amt. of Divd. $	Date Decl.	Ex-divd. Date	Stock of Record	Payment Date
0.14	Jul. 2	Jul. 10	Jul. 16	Jul. 31'84
0.14	Oct. 16	Oct. 22	Oct. 26	Oct. 31'84
5-for-4	Oct. 16	Dec. 3	Nov. 16	Nov. 30'84
0.14	Jan. 8	Jan. 14	Jan. 21	Jan. 31'85
0.14	Apr. 1	Apr. 9	Apr. 15	Apr. 30'85

Capitalization

Long Term Debt: $42,436,406 (3/85), incl. $10 million of 8¼% Eurodollar debs. conv. into com. at $12.96 per sh.

Minority Interest: $713,401 (8/84).

Common Stock: 9,631,868 shs. (no par). Officers & directors own about 10%, incl. some 6% owned by T. C. Sullivan and related trusts. Institutions hold about 17%. Shareholders: 4,290 of record (7/84).

Office—2628 Pearl Rd., P.O. Box 777, Medina, Ohio 44258. **Tel**—(216) 225-3192. **Chrmn & CEO**—T. C. Sullivan. **Pres**—J. A. Karman. **Exec VP**—J. H. Morris. **VP & Secy**—J. K. Nemeth. **VP & Treas**—R. E. Klar. **Dirs**—C. M. Blair, L. E. Gigax, N. H. Hammink, L. C. Jones, J. A. Karman, D. K. Miller, J. H. Morris, J. K. Nemeth, K. O'Donnell, W. A. Papenbrock, T. C. Sullivan. **Transfer Agents**—National City Bank, Cleveland; Chase Manhattan Bank, NYC. **Incorporated** in Ohio in 1947.

Information has been obtained from sources believed to be reliable, but its accuracy and completeness are not guaranteed.   Richard M. Levine

Figure 8-3   Side two of the same Standard & Poor's report.

is higher. A personal investor, of course, is free to do as he or she chooses, but there are good reasons for conservatism in this area, as you'll learn.

I'm now ready to begin the most important part of my analysis, filling out the Stock Selection Guide.

THE STOCK SELECTION GUIDE

The Stock Selection Guide is one of the most useful forms printed and sold by the N.A.I.C. to its members. Developed over many years, it has become the one tool most used by all investment clubs and the one often cited by clubs as the reason for their success. The Guide costs mere pennies to buy and is so helpful that I recommend it to non–club members as well.

It's an 8½- by 11-inch sheet of paper printed on both sides (see Figures 8-4 and 8-5) and provides a way to determine when and if a stock should be purchased. Prior to the appearance of the Guide, both investment clubs and individuals undoubtedly found stock analysis a formidable task. Although there's plenty of information around, interpreting that information, boiling it down to a buy or don't buy decision, hasn't been easy.

The annual report of the company contains balance sheets and income statements, full of numbers which may mean little or nothing to you as an investing novice. The written material may be even more confusing, and as it's prepared by officers of the company, it could be somewhat biased in its approach. Even the Value Line and Standard & Poor's reports, although objective, are filled with numbers whose significance may be a mystery. But the Stock Selection Guide uses the numbers to point the way toward a decision and, if you take the time to understand it, leaves you considerably wiser about the company than when you started.

Bearing in mind that you're looking for growth stocks (those that will show a total return of about 15 percent a year), you want to know if the price of the stock appreciates sufficiently every year and if its dividends increase enough periodically to bring about that return. Of course, you can't really see into the future, but you can investigate the past performance of the company; and if that performance is within your guidelines, you can presume the company may continue growing.

Price appreciation is a product of how much the public is willing to pay for the stock; stock prices rise when there's more demand to buy than to sell and decline when the opposite is true.

STOCK SELECTION GUIDE	NATIONAL ASSOCIATION OF INVESTORS CORPORATION **NAIC** INVESTMENT EDUCATION SINCE 1951	Company _____ Date _____

The most widely used aid
to good investment judgment

| Prepared by_____Data taken from_____ |
| Where traded _____ Major product/service _____ |

CAPITALIZATION	Authorized	Outstanding
Preferred		
Common		
Other Debt	Potential Dilution	

1 VISUAL ANALYSIS of Sales, Earnings and Price

RECENT QUARTERLY FIGURES

	SALES	EARNINGS PER SHARE
Latest Quarter		
Year Ago Quarter		
Percentage Change		

See Section III, Chapters 2, 3 and 4 of Investors Manual for Complete instructions. Use this guide as working section of NAIC Stock Selection Guide and Report.

(1) Historical Sales Growth _____ %
(2) Estimated Future Sales Growth _____ %
(3) Historical Earnings Per Share Growth _____ %
(4) Estimated Future Earnings Per Share Growth _____ %

Figure 8-4   Side one of the N.A.I.C. Stock Selection Guide.

The demand is created when the public is optimistic about the
company. This optimism, in turn, is created by positive features,
such as steadily increasing sales, earnings, dividends, book value,
return on equity, and pre-tax profit, all of which I'll explain thoroughly
later.

2 EVALUATING MANAGEMENT   Company _____

	19___	19___	19___	19___	19___	19___	19___	19___	19___	19___	LAST 5 YEAR AVE.	TREND UP	TREND DOWN
A % Pre-tax Profit on Sales (Net Before Taxes ÷ Sales)													
B % Earned on Invested Capital (E/S ÷ Book Value)													

3 PRICE-EARNINGS HISTORY as an indicator of the future

PRESENT PRICE_____   HIGH THIS YEAR_____   LOW THIS YEAR_____

Year	A PRICE HIGH	B PRICE LOW	C Earnings Per Share	D Price Earnings Ratio HIGH A ÷ C	E Price Earnings Ratio LOW B ÷ C	F Dividend Per Share	G % Payout F ÷ C X 100	H % High Yield F ÷ B X 100
1								
2								
3								
4								
5								
6 TOTAL								
7 AVERAGE								
8 AVERAGE PRICE EARNINGS RATIO				9 CURRENT PRICE EARNINGS RATIO				

4 EVALUATING RISK and REWARD over the next 5 years

A HIGH PRICE — NEXT 5 YEARS
Avg. High P/E _____ (3D7) x Estimated High Earnings/Share _____ = Forecast High Price B-1 $_____ (4A1)

B LOW PRICE — NEXT 5 YEARS
(a) Avg. Low P/E _____ (3E7) x Estimated Low E/Share _____ = $_____
(b) Avg. Low Price of Last 5 Years = _____ (3B7)
(c) Recent Severe Market Low Price = _____
(d) Price Dividend Will Support $\frac{\text{Present Divd.}}{\text{High Yield}}$ (H) = _____ = _____
Selected Estimated Low Price _____ B-2 $_____ (4B1)

C ZONING
_____ (4A1) High Forecast Price Minus _____ (4B1) Low Forecast Price Equals _____ (C) Range. ⅓ of Range. = _____ (4CD)
Lower ⅓ = _____ (4B1) To _____ (Buy) (4C2)
Middle ⅓ = _____ To _____ (Maybe) (4C3)
Upper ⅓ = _____ To _____ (4A1) (Sell) (4C4)
Present Market Price of _____ is in the _____ (4C5) Range

D UP-SIDE DOWN-SIDE RATIO (Potential Gain vs. Risk of Loss)
High Price _____ (4A1) Minus Present Price _____
_____ = _____ = _____ (4D) To 1
Present Price _____ Minus Low Price _____ (4B1)

5 5-YEAR POTENTIAL

A Present Full Year's Dividend $_____
_____ = _____ x 100 = _____ Present Yield or % Returned on Purchase Price
Present Price of Stock $_____
B AVERAGE YIELD OVER NEXT 5 YEARS
Avg. Earn. Per Share Next 5 Years _____ x Avg. % Payout _____ (3G7) = _____ %
Present Price $_____

Figure 8-5   Side two of the Stock Selection Guide.

But finding a superior company is only half the battle; the other half is to find one that's reasonably priced. If you purchased an expensive automobile, you'd feel cheated if you paid twice as much for it as someone who bought the identical car from a different dealer. So, too, in the stock market, you don't want to pay

$50 per share for a stock that someone else paid only $10 for a year ago, or will pay $10 for six months from now. This second criterion for finding the right stock to buy is also considered when filling out the Stock Selection Guide.

The next chapter will take you step by step through this process, and Chapter 10 will discuss each point in detail, explaining what the numbers mean and how they relate to your decision-making.

Filling Out the Stock Selection Guide 9

This chapter will duplicate some of the information found in the N.A.I.C. *Investor's Manual,* but my emphasis here will be on my own club's analysis system. For those who don't own the *Investor's Manual,* this will be a detailed lesson in filling out the Guide. To make it even easier, we'll go step by step, filling it out for a specific company, RPM, Inc., traded over the counter.

HEADING

Begin at the top of side one with the heading. Fill in the current date and your initials where indicated. Then, using the information from the Value Line report (marked with arrows in Figure 9-1), fill in the blanks in Figure 9-2.

RECENT QUARTERLY SALES

The next section of the Guide (see Figure 9-3) is numbered 1 and is called Visual Analysis. It consists of a logarithmic chart with space for fifteen years' data. In the box in the upper left corner (see Figure 9-4) record sales and earnings of the company for the most recent quarter and for the same quarter of the previous year. Find this

Company Name   Where Traded   Price   P/E Ratio   Yield

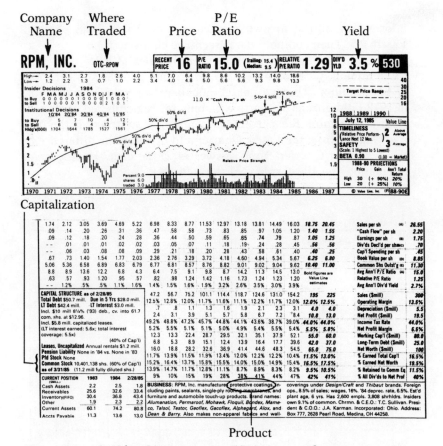

Capitalization

Product

Figure 9-1 A Value Line report on RPM, Inc., with company name, exchange where traded, price, P/E ratio, yield, capitalization and product indicated.

Figure 9-2 A section of side one of the Stock Selection Guide, filled out for RPM, Inc.

information at the arrows marked on the Value Line sheet in Figure 9-5. Then compute the percentage changes.

In our example, the latest quarterly sales of RPM, Inc. were $39.8 million, whereas a year ago, the same quarter showed sales of $31.3 million. Using a pocket calculator (or your long division; in 1972 I did dozens of charts with only my remembered arithmetic skills), determine the percentage change by subtracting the Year Ago Quarter from the Latest Quarter and dividing the difference by the Year Ago Quarter. Your answer is 27 percent. Do the same calculations for the earnings of the company.

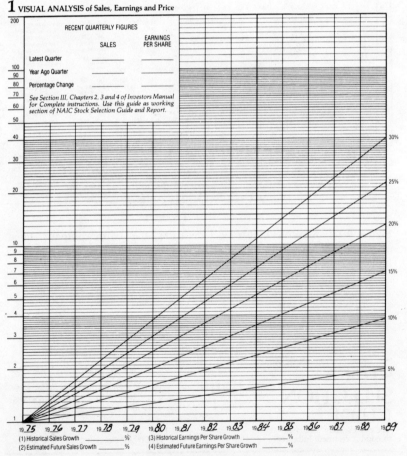

Figure 9-3   A section of side one of the Stock Selection Guide showing the Visual Analysis chart, with dates inserted at the bottom.

1 VISUAL ANALYSIS of Sales, Earnings and Price

RECENT QUARTERLY FIGURES

	SALES	EARNINGS PER SHARE
Latest Quarter	$39.8 mil.	.10
Year Ago Quarter	31.3	.08
Percentage Change	+27%	+25%

See Section III, Chapters 2, 3 and 4 of Investors Manual for Complete instructions. Use this guide as working section of NAIC Stock Selection Guide and Report.

Figure 9-4   A section of side one of the Stock Selection Guide showing the Recent Quarterly Figures, filled in for RPM, Inc.

VISUAL ANALYSIS

Enter the dates at the bottom of the chart in Figure 9-3. Notice a slightly darker vertical line two-thirds to the right on the chart. Number this line with the date of the last complete year for which you have data for the company. In this example, you are filling it out in 1985, and you have current information for 1984. Then go backward, to the left along the chart, and fill in the previous nine years' dates, in this case ending with 1975 on the first vertical line. From that darker line date the ones to the right successively, ending with 1989.

The three statistics entered on this chart are price motion of

Quarterly Sales & Earnings

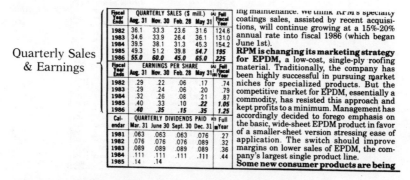

Fiscal Year Ends	QUARTERLY SALES ($ mill.)				(A) Full Fiscal Year
	Aug. 31	Nov. 30	Feb. 28	May 31	
1982	36.1	33.3	23.6	31.6	124.6
1983	34.6	33.9	26.4	36.1	131.0
1984	39.5	38.1	31.3	45.3	154.2
1985	49.3	51.2	39.8	54.7	195
1986	55.0	60.0	45.0	65.0	225

Fiscal Year Ends	EARNINGS PER SHARE				(A) Full Fiscal Year
	Aug. 31	Nov. 30	Feb. 28	May 31	
1982	.29	.22	.06	.17	.74
1983	.29	.24	.06	.20	.79
1984	.32	.26	.08	.21	.87
1985	.40	.33	.10	.22	1.05
1986	.40	.35	.15	.35	1.25

Cal-endar	QUARTERLY DIVIDENDS PAID				(B) Full Year
	Mar. 31	June 30	Sept. 30	Dec. 31	
1981	.063	.063	.063	.076	.27
1982	.076	.076	.076	.089	.32
1983	.089	.089	.089	.089	.36
1984	.111	.111	.111	.111	.44
1985	.14	.14			

ing maintenance. We think RPM's specialty coatings sales, assisted by recent acquisitions, will continue growing at a 15%-20% annual rate into fiscal 1986 (which began June 1st).

RPM is changing its marketing strategy for EPDM, a low-cost, single-ply roofing material. Traditionally, the company has been highly successful in pursuing market niches for specialized products. But the competitive market for EPDM, essentially a commodity, has resisted this approach and kept profits to a minimum. Management has accordingly decided to forego emphasis on the basic, wide-sheet EPDM product in favor of a smaller-sheet version stressing ease of application. The switch should improve margins on lower sales of EPDM, the company's largest single product line.
Some new consumer products are being

Figure 9-5   A Value Line Report on RPM, Inc., with the section showing Quarterly Sales and Earnings Per Share indicated.

the shares, gross sales (sometimes called revenues), and earnings per share. Use three different colored pencils or pens for this data. I use a black felt-tip pen for price, blue pencil for sales, and red pencil for earnings; any system will do. (*Note:* because color could not be printed in the figures shown in this book, we have indicated on each graph the color(s) you should use.)

Before entering numbers, it's important to glance over the entire ten years' statistics to determine the scope. This will enable you to draw your lines in the best position for analysis.

The Stock Selection Guide uses a logarithmic scale, with the first number always 1 (one), not 0 (zero). The vertical axis is labeled 1 to 10, 10 to 100, and so on, each "cycle" taking the same vertical distance. Because of its unique scale, the chart allows the same percentage change be registered by the same vertical distance, regardless of the actual numbers involved.

Looking at the Value Line report on RPM, Inc. (Figure 9-6), you see that during the past ten years, sales have gone from $35 million to $154 million. Therefore you will place a blue dot on the vertical line representing the year 1975 where it intersects with the horizontal line representing 35 (in this case, halfway between the 3 and the 4 on the lefthand scale). The upper cycle (between the 30 and the 40) could have been used, but that would not have left sufficient room for the data in later years.

Continue placing dots on appropriate lines for the remaining

1975	1976	1977	1978	1979	1980	1981	1982	1983	1984	1985	1986	1987	© Value Line, Inc. (F)	88-90E
5.22	6.98	8.33	8.77	11.53	12.97	13.18	13.81	14.49	16.03	**18.75**	**20.45**		Sales per sh (A)	**26.55**
.36	.47	.58	.58	.73	.83	.85	.97	1.05	1.20	**1.40**	**1.55**		"Cash Flow" per sh	**2.20**
.28	.36	.44	.50	.59	.65	.65	.74	.79	.87	**1.05**	**1.25**		Earnings per sh (B)	**1.75**
.02	.03	.05	.07	.11	.18	.19	.24	.28	.45	**.56**	**.56**		Div'ds Decl'd per sh(C)	**.70**
.09	.29	.21	.18	.20	.28	.43	.58	.61	.40	**.40**	**.25**		Cap'l Spending per sh	**.45**
2.03	2.36	2.76	3.29	3.72	4.18	4.60	4.94	5.34	5.67	**6.25**	**6.80**		Book Value per sh (D)	**8.85**
6.79	6.77	6.81	8.57	8.76	8.82	9.01	9.02	9.04	9.62	**10.40**	**11.00**		Common Shs Outst'g (E)	**11.30**
4.3	6.4	7.5	9.1	9.8	8.7	14.2	11.3	14.5	13.0	Bold figures are			Avg Ann'l P/E Ratio (A)	**15.0**
.57	.82	.98	1.24	1.42	1.16	1.73	1.24	1.23	1.20	Value Line			Relative P/E Ratio	**1.25**
1.6%	1.4%	1.5%	1.6%	1.9%	3.2%	2.6%	3.5%	3.0%	3.9%	estimates			Avg Ann'l Div'd Yield	**2.7%**
35.4	47.2	56.7	75.2	101.1	114.4	118.7	124.6	131.0	154.2	**195**	**225**		Sales ($mill)	**300**
1.54	12.5%	12.8%	12.0%	11.7%	11.6%	11.1%	12.2%	11.7%	12.0%	**12.0%**	**12.5%**		Operating Margin	**13.5%**
*),	.7	.8	1.1	1.3	1.6	1.9	2.1	2.3	3.1	**4.0**	**4.0**		Depreciation ($mill)	**5.5**
61.7	2.4	3.1	3.9	5.1	5.7	5.8	6.7	7.2	8.4	**10.8**	**13.0**		Net Profit ($mill)	**19.5**
	49.2%	48.8%	47.2%	45.7%	44.8%	44.1%	43.6%	38.7%	39.0%	**44.0%**	**44.0%**		Income Tax Rate	**44.0%**
	5.2%	5.5%	5.1%	5.1%	5.0%	4.9%	5.4%	5.5%	5.4%	**5.5%**	**5.8%**		Net Profit Margin	**6.5%**
	12.3	13.3	22.4	28.7	29.5	32.1	35.1	37.9	52.1	**55.0**	**60.0**		Working Cap'l ($mill)	**80.0**
ap'l)	6.8	5.3	8.9	15.1	12.4	13.9	16.4	17.7	39.6	**42.0**	**37.0**		Long-Term Debt ($mill)	**25.0**
mill.	16.0	18.8	28.2	32.6	36.9	41.4	44.6	48.3	54.5	**65.0**	**75.0**		Net Worth ($mill)	**100**
'83	11.7%	13.9%	11.5%	11.9%	13.4%	12.0%	12.2%	12.2%	10.4%	**11.5%**	**13.0%**		% Earned Total Cap'l	**16.5%**
:ap'l)	15.2%	16.4%	13.7%	15.8%	15.5%	14.0%	15.0%	14.9%	15.4%	**16.5%**	**17.5%**		% Earned Net Worth	**19.5%**
i.)	13.9%	14.7%	11.7%	12.8%	11.1%	8.7%	8.9%	8.3%	8.2%	**9.5%**	**10.5%**		% Retained to Comm Eq	**11.5%**
/28/85	9%	10%	15%	19%	28%	38%	41%	44%	47%	**42%**	**41%**		% All Div'ds to Net Prof	**40%**

◄── Earnings
◄── Sales

Figure 9-6 Value Line Report on RPM, Inc. with Annual Sales and Earnings Per Share indicated.

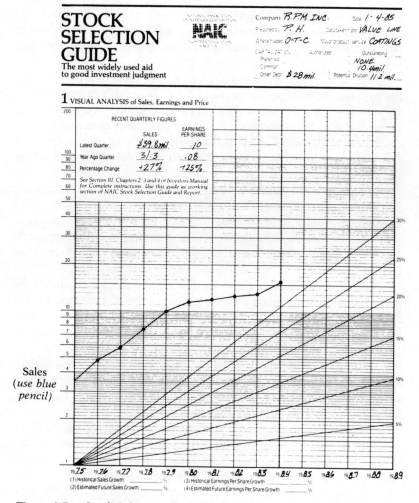

Figure 9-7   Stock Selection Guide for RPM, Inc., showing ten-year sales line drawn on the chart.

nine years and draw a solid blue line connecting them, as shown in Figure 9-7.

Notice that when you got to 1979, the figures were over $100 million. That amount is represented by the 10 in the lefthand scale. The 20, ten lines above that, represents $200 million. The number 200 at the top of the scale represents ten times that, or $2 billion. If RPM had increased its sales to over $2 billion, you can see there wouldn't be room on this chart to handle it. The numbers can be made to represent anything you choose—one, ten, one hundred, one thousand, or whatever, provided you remember the relationship between them, as you'll see when you enter the earnings per share.

The next thing you want to chart about sales is the trend over the past ten years. If you have the N.A.I.C. *Investor's Manual,* you'll see that it suggests a few ways to draw a trend line, one of which is called the Mid-Point Method. Since my club uses this method, I'll describe it; but you should read about the others. If you are in a club, discuss the various methods with club members and adopt the one the majority prefers.

The Mid-Point Method is mathematical. Using your calculator, add the sales figures for the first five years (in the example, 1975 through 1979) and divide by five. You now have an average for these years. Enter this on the chart by making a small **x** at the appropriate place on the vertical line which is in the middle of that five-year span, 1977.

Now add the sales figures for the second five years, divide by five, and enter this average with an **x** on the vertical line representing the year 1982. Using a ruler, connect the two **x**s with a dotted blue line that goes all the way across the chart, from 1975 on the left to 1989 on the right (see Figure 9-8).

Measure the distance from the beginning of the trend line to the bottom of the chart; in the case of RPM, it's 2¼ inches. Then mark down 2¼ inches from the end of the trend line. The point indicated shows the percentage growth.

The slanted lines printed on the chart and labeled on the right range from 5 to 30 percent. If the trend line you drew matches one of these, it will tell you the exact rate of growth of the company being studied. In the case of RPM, the mark you made at the right edge of the chart fell just above 15 percent, indicating a ten-year sales growth rate of about 16 percent. Enter this figure in the space provided at the bottom of the chart, marked Historical Sales Growth. You may also enter 16 percent in "Estimated Future Sales Growth," unless the trend line has been adjusted, in which case the adjusted figure is entered. See the next section, on Earnings Per Share, to learn why and how trend lines may be adjusted.

Next, move on to earnings per share. Using the figures on the Value Line report (indicated by arrows on Figure 9-6) and the same technique you used for sales (except for switching to your red pencil), place your dots and draw a solid red line for ten years' earnings figures.

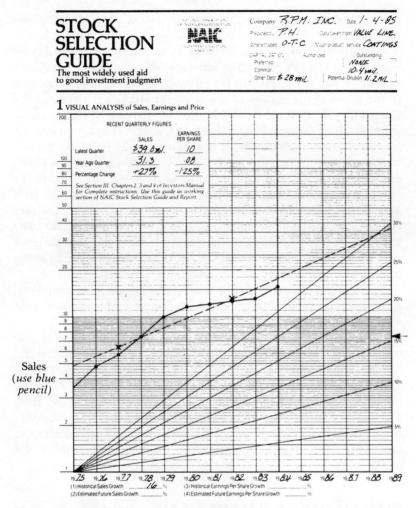

Figure 9-8   Stock Selection Guide for RPM, Inc., showing sales and sales trend line, and indicating Historical Sales Growth.

Notice that earnings for RPM grew from $0.28 per share in 1975 to $0.87 in 1984, yet you placed the dots in the same section (cycle) of the chart as when you were using millions of dollars. For the sake of your analysis, the 3 on the lefthand scale is not read as $30 million but 30 cents, and the 10 is not $100 million, but $1. You can do this because, as stated earlier, the numbers can mean anything you wish. You're concerned with the relationships between the numbers rather than the numbers themselves.

Draw a trend line for earnings in the same way you did for sales, using the Mid-Point Method or whatever method you chose. Determine the rate of growth for earnings, and put this information in the space at the bottom of the chart for Historical Earnings Per Share Growth. Enter the same figures for Estimated Future Earnings Per Share Growth (Figure 9-9). In the next chapter I'll discuss how to adjust these numbers if necessary.

The final data to enter on this side of the Stock Selection Guide are the price variations. This information is found at the top of the chart on the Value Line report, and in Figure 9-10 it's marked with arrows. Using a black felt-tip pen, draw a vertical line over (or very close to) the vertical line representing each of the past ten years, the top of your line beginning at the point marking the highest price paid for the stock that year and the bottom of the line ending at the point marking the lowest price (see Figure 9-11).

Label the chart, showing what the colored lines represent. Now turn over the Stock Selection Guide and continue your analysis.

Notice that on this side you'll do many calculations. For ease in handling the figures and to save time, round them off to the nearest whole number. The difference between profit margins of 12.4 and 12 percent is miniscule for our purposes, so use 12. Round off prices (unless you're considering stocks selling at less than $10 per share) to the nearest dollar. This evaluation process is not a mathematical drill, after all. Your judgment will determine the worth of a stock, not whether its average P/E ratio is 9.8 or 10.

EVALUATING MANAGEMENT

Section 2 at the top is titled "Evaluating Management." Write in the name of the company on the top line. Underneath is a table divided into two sections: **A,** Percent Pre-Tax Profit on Sales, and **B,** Percent Earned on Invested Capital. Across the top of the table are spaces for you to enter the dates for the past ten years.

The way to calculate the numbers you'll put in these boxes is described underneath each title. Under **A,** in parentheses, you find: Net Before Taxes Divided by Sales. Under **B,** you see: E/S (Earnings per Share) Divided by Book Value.

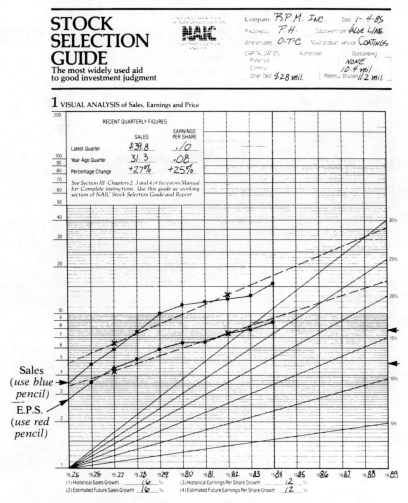

Figure 9-9   Stock Selection Guide for RPM, Inc., showing Sales and Sales Trend Line, and Earnings Per Share and Earnings trend line.

While the Standard & Poor's report contains a column labeled Net Before Taxes (Figure 9-12), the Value Line report does not, so you must calculate this figure before dividing it by Sales. Following the arrows I marked on Figure 9-13, find the necessary numbers; then subtract the Income Tax Rate from 100 and divide the Net Profit figure by the difference. For example, the 1984 figures for RPM would produce the following equation:

High & Low Prices Last 10 Years

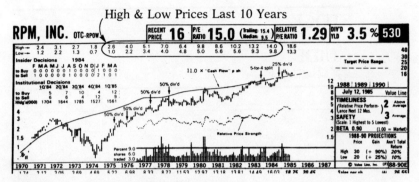

Figure 9-10   Value Line Report on RPM, Inc., with High and Low Prices for the last 10 years indicated.

$$\$8.4 \text{ million} \div (100 - 39\%) = \$13.7 \text{ million}$$

You now have the Net Before Taxes figure and can divide that by Sales.

Although finding the value of **A** is a little more difficult with the Value Line report, this report provides a shortcut for item **B**. Rather than divide Earnings Per Share by Book Value, use the figure in Value Line's Percent Earned Net Worth column, as the figures are the same.

At the end of the columns in Section **2** is a box marked Last 5 Year Average and you enter here the number you get from adding the last five years (1980 through 1984) and dividing by five. You are to judge whether this five-year trend is up or down. In the case of RPM, it's actually flat (see Figure 9-14).

PRICE/EARNINGS HISTORY

The first data to enter under **3**, Price/Earnings History (Figure 9-15), are the current price of the stock and its high and low price over the past fifty-two weeks. This is where *Barron's* or your other newspaper is used. (See Figure 9-16 for the relevant section of a newspaper stock page.) As you see, the fifty-two-week high and low are listed at the extreme left end of the line for the stock listing. For present price, use the one in the column marked Last.

In the table in Section **3** enter dates (1980 through 1984) in the column marked Year, then the high and low prices of the stock for those years. Add all the low prices in column B, enter that sum in the box marked Total, then divide by five and enter *that* number in the box marked Average.

Enter earnings per share for each of the five years in column C, then calculate the high and low price/earnings ratios. You remem-

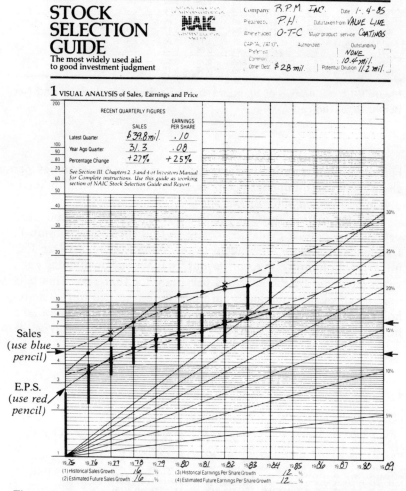

Figure 9-11   Stock Selection Guide for RPM, Inc., showing Sales, Sales Trend Line, Earnings, Earnings Trend Line, and vertical lines indicating rice Range for the past ten years.

Sales   Net Before Taxes

5052   RPM, Inc.

Income Data (Million $)

Year Ended May 31	Oper. Revs.	Oper. Inc.	% Oper. Inc. of Revs.	Cap. Exp.	Depr.	Int. Exp.	Net Bef. Taxes	Eff. Tax Rate	Net Inc.	% Net Inc. of Revs.
1984	154	18.5	12.0%	3.80	3.37	3.18	13.7	38.9%	8.38	5.4%
1983	131	15.3	11.7%	5.49	2.33	2.46	³11.9	38.7%	7.17	5.5%
1982	125	15.2	12.2%	5.22	2.09	2.32	³11.8	43.6%	⁴6.68	5.4%
1981	119	13.2	11.1%	3.85	1.89	1.88	10.7	44.2%	5.81	4.9%
¹1980	114	13.2	11.6%	2.49	1.60	1.89	10.5	44.8%	5.71	4.0%
1979	101	11.8	11.7%	4.59	1.28	1.17	9.8	45.7%	5.14	5.1%
¹1978	75	9.1	12.1%	1.55	1.11	0.90	7.3	47.3%	3.85	5.1%
¹1977	57	7.3	12.8%	1.41	0.84	0.55	6.0	48.7%	3.09	5.5%
1976	47	5.9	12.5%	2.55	0.75	0.56	4.8	49.1%	2.43	5.2%
¹1975	35	4.5	12.8%	0.60	0.58	0.46	3.6	48.3%	1.87	5.3%

Figure 9-12   Side two of Standard & Poor's Report with Sales and Net Before Taxes indicated.

ber you get these ratios by dividing the price by the earnings per share. Add the numbers in column D and enter the sum in Total; divide by five and enter in Average.

So far in this section, you've entered figures that you used before, so I haven't explained where to find them. For column F, Dividends Per Share, turn again to the Value Line report (see Figure 9-17). Column G, Percent Payout, is filled out by dividing each year's dividend by the earnings per share for that year. This tells how much of the company's earnings were returned to the shareholders in the form of dividends each year. Add all the numbers in this column to get the Total and divide by five to arrive at

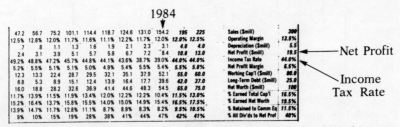

Figure 9-13   Value Line Report on RPM, Inc., with Net Profit and Income Tax Rate indicated.

2 EVALUATING MANAGEMENT   Company___*R. P. M. INC.*_____

	19_75_	19_76_	19_77_	19_78_	19_79_	19_80_	19_81_	19_82_	19_83_	19_84_	LAST 5 YEAR AVE.	TREND UP	DOWN
A % Pre-tax Profit on Sales (Net Before Taxes ÷ Sales)	10	10	11	10	10	9	9	9	9	9	9	FLAT	
B % Earned on Invested Capital (E/S ÷ Book Value)	13	15	16	15	16	15	14	15	15	15	15	FLAT	

Figure 9-14   Side two of Stock Selection Guide for RPM, Inc., filled in with calculations with which to evaluate management.

the Average; enter these figures in the appropriate boxes. (see Figure 9-15.)

Column H, Percent High Yield, is calculated by dividing the dividend by the low price for that year. Yield is like interest on your money. If you had bought the stock at the low for the year, you would have paid $5.00 per share for the stock in 1980, and since the company returned $0.18 cents to you in the form of dividends, your yield on that investment would have been 3.6 percent.

At the bottom of this section, Line 8, you're to calculate the average Price/Earnings Ratio. This is done by adding the high P/E ratio over the past five years (column D) to the low for the same period (column E) and dividing by two.

Then you enter the current P/E ratio. To get this, you can divide the current price by the latest full-year's per-share earnings; however, rather than doing this yourself, use the figure given in the newspaper's stock tables (see Figure 9-16).

3 PRICE-EARNINGS HISTORY as an indicator of the future

PRESENT PRICE ___13___   HIGH THIS YEAR ___14___   LOW THIS YEAR ___10___

Year	A PRICE HIGH	B PRICE LOW	C Earnings Per Share	D Price Earnings Ratio HIGH A ÷ C	E Price Earnings Ratio LOW B ÷ C	F Dividend Per Share	G % Payout F ÷ C X 100	H % High Yield F ÷ B X 100
1 1980	10	5	.65	15	8	.18	28	3.6
2 1981	9	6	.65	14	9	.19	29	3.2
3 1982	10	6	.74	14	8	.24	32	4.0
4 1983	13	9	.79	16	11	.28	35	3.1
5 1984	14	10	.87	16	11	.45	52	4.5
6 TOTAL		36		75	47		176	
7 AVERAGE		7		15	9		35	
8 AVERAGE PRICE EARNINGS RATIO			12		9 CURRENT PRICE EARNINGS RATIO	12		

Figure 9-15   Section of side two of Stock Selection Guide on RPM, Inc., filled in with calculations to show the Price/Earnings History.

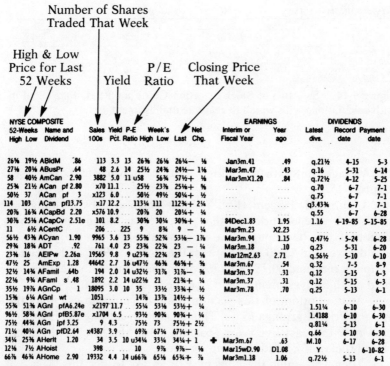

Figure 9-16 Section of newspaper stock pages, showing High & Low Prices for the last fifty-two weeks, Number of Shares Traded, Yield, P/E Ratios and Closing Prices for the week.

The quoted P/E Ratio is more accurate, particularly if your calculations are made late in the calendar year, because the newspaper figures usually use the latest four-quarter earnings, not the company's last complete fiscal year earnings.

EVALUATING RISK AND REWARD

Section **4,** Evaluating Risk and Reward Over the Next 5 Years (see Figure 9-18), may look more difficult than it is. Part **A** merely requires you to enter the Average High P/E (box D-7 in the Price/Earnings History table, Figure 9-15) and multiply it by the estimated high earnings per share five years into the future to produce a Forecast High Price.

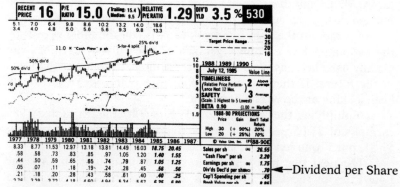

◄──Dividend per Share

Figure 9-17   Value Line Report on RPM, Inc., with Dividends Per Share indicated.

The second number comes from side one of the Stock Selection Guide. Turn the Guide over and determine the point at which your earnings trend line intersects with the last vertical line on the chart—1989—and read it in terms of dollars. In the case of RPM stock, the trend line touches the right edge at about $1.70 per share. Multiplying the Average High P/E by $1.70 per share gives you a Forecast High Price of $26, which is what you hope the stock will be worth five years from now.

Part **B** provides a low price estimate for five years into the

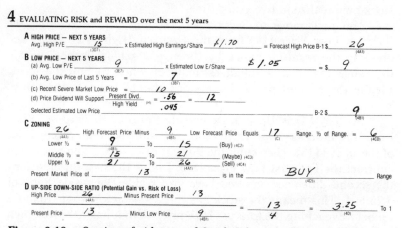

Figure 9-18   Section of side two of Stock Selection Guide on RPM, Inc., showing calculations to determine Risk and Reward over the next five years.

future. Four numbers create this forecast low price. The first, marked (a), is calculated by multiplying the average low price/earnings ratio of the past five years (box E-7 in the table above) by the estimated low earnings per share. The current earnings are usually used here, as we don't expect earnings to go lower than this in the future. If they do decline past that point, we've obviously been looking at the wrong company.

Multiplying the Average Low P/E of 9 by the estimated 1985 earnings of $1.05 per share, you arrive at a price of $9. (Actually $9.81, but I rounded it off, since these are only estimates.)

The next two numbers are historical in nature; (b) Average Low Price of the Last Five Years, as indicated in Section **3** and (c) Recent Severe Market Low, which I consider to be the lowest price paid within the past fifty-two weeks, as indicated by your newspaper stock tables. (Another interpretation is to use the lowest price of the past five years.)

The last, (d) Price Dividend Will Support, is determined by dividing the current dividend by the highest yield in the past five years. Rather than using the 1984 dividend, however, you should use the dividend given in the newspaper stock tables or the one Value Line estimates will be the dividend in 1985.

You now have four numbers (three if the stock pays no dividends) from which to arrive at a logical price. You can do it simply by adding the four numbers and dividing by four to reach this decision. (Again, round it to the nearest dollar.) With the help of the Guide, you have now arrived at the high and low price limits the stock may realize in five years' time.

You now move to Section **4-C,** Zoning. By subtracting the Forecast Low Price ($9) from the Forecast High Price ($26) and dividing the resulting range by three, you set up "zones" within the range that give a rough estimate of when to buy the stock. Ideally the current price of the stock should fall into the "Buy" zone.

Section **4-D** is Up-side Down-side Ratio or Reward vs. Risk. Enter the Forecast High Price ($26) and subtract the Present Price of the stock ($13). Then enter the Present Price on the line below and subtract the Forecast Low Price ($9). Divide the first difference by the second difference and you have an Up-side Down-side Ratio of 3.25 to 1. This means the stock has three times more room to move up before reaching the forecast high price than it has to move down before reaching the forecast low price. Such a ratio indicates that it is a good time to buy because most of the hoped-for appreciation is yet to come.

FIVE-YEAR POTENTIAL

Section **5**, Five-Year Potential (Figure 9–19), is concerned with yield. (Naturally, if the company pays no dividend, you skip it.) **A** in this section shows the Present Yield by asking you to divide the Present Full Year Dividend by the Present Price of Stock. This number multiplied by 100 shows a return of 3.5 percent.

   B in this section calculates the average yield from the stock over the next five years. To calculate **B**, turn over the Stock Selection Guide (or turn to Figure 9-9). Find the point where the Earnings Per Share trend line is crossed by the vertical line representing the midpoint of the time period of the future five-year trend, or the line labelled 1987. The horizontal line crossing that point represents the dollar value of the average earning per share (in the case of RPM, Inc., about $1.30). This is multiplied by the Average Percent Payout of 35 percent (from box G-7 of Section 3; as shown in Figure 9-15) and divided by the present price of the stock, resulting in a figure of 3.5 percent. This percentage tells you what yield you might expect to average over the next five years, if you were to buy the stock at its current price.

COMPUTER HELP

Not everyone finds the Stock Selection Guide easy to understand and to do. For some this can be a problem great enough to put them off from this important task altogether. If you're one of these people, there is a solution, provided you have a personal computer at your disposal.

   The computerization of the Stock Selection Guide is a mixed blessing; there is a real benefit from doing a Guide by hand. Doing so not only requires you to understand the interrelationships between the various numbers, but helps you get a feel for the numbers

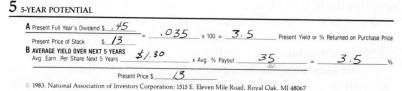

Figure 9-19   Section of side two of Stock Selection Guide for RPM, Inc., showing calculations to determine Five-Year Yield Potential.

themselves. This can be important when it comes to comparing one stock with another, or to others within an industry. However, if one doesn't do Guides anyway out of fear or misunderstanding, he or she can only benefit from using a computer.

I recommend that everyone start out doing Guides by hand so that the necessary understanding is developed; then move on to a computer to improve the quantity and quality of analysis. A strong benefit accruing to those who use a computer is that it allows more studies to be accomplished in a given amount of time.

Everything else being equal, more is definitely better: the more stocks you study, the more likely you will be to find those stocks that meet your criteria. With a computer, the number of stocks studied can be increased by 400 percent or more, which should result in finding a greater number of suitable investments.

There are a number of computer programs on the market with which you can use the Stock Selection Guide. Some of these are advertised in *Better Investing* magazine, but I can't comment on these because I personally haven't used them. Since the procedure for calculating the guide is standardized by the N.A.I.C., most programs should be arithmetically correct and will vary primarily in the details of input, output, ease of operation, and equipment required.

It is important that the program you choose allows you to interact with the results, so that you can change some of the important numbers and compare the different results. The N.A.I.C. emphasizes the importance of this interaction. Although the Guide bases its predictions for the future on what took place in the past, the past is not always that good a predictor of things to come. If you feel that you have better information (or intuition) than history provides, you should inject this into the Guide, whether it's done manually or by computer.

Probably the most important example is in the projection of future earnings per share. You must be allowed to put your own best judgment into this estimate. The program I use (and recommend) provides the best of both worlds; it makes its own projections based on the numbers I provide from my statistics, shows me the results both numerically and graphically, then invites me to change its predictions if I think I can do better.

This program, which is produced by a firm with which I have some affiliation, works best for me because I had some influence on the way it was designed; I made the maker do it my way! Here's how it works:

When I start the program, it leads me through two "screens" of data input, equivalent to filling out the front of the Guide. I don't have to do any graphing, just input the raw numbers (historical sales, earnings per share, prices, dividends, and such). It takes about five or ten minutes to key in this data. However, about three seconds after I'm through, *the program* is through, saving me at least a half hour per study.

First, the computer program presents a one-screen summary of the results of its computations, listing all the important ones, including whether the stock is in the Buy, Maybe, or Sell range (see Figure 9-20). It also shows which of the results meet certain criteria

```
NATIONAL  ASSOCIATION  OF  INVESTMENT  CLUBS

S T O C K     S E L E C T I O N     G U I D E


==================================================
        COMPANY NAME: High Voltage Engineering
           EXCHANGE: NYSE
        STOCK SYMBOL: HVE
        MAJOR PRODUCT: Electrical Insulation Products
==================================================
```

```
          A N A L Y S I S    S U M M A R Y

 - Given the current data, this stock is in the  BUY range
 - Positive factors exceed negative factors by   7 to 3

   QUICK REVIEW:                                        POS/NEG

 - Last quarter's SALES compared to a year ago:    1.6%     +
 - Last quarter's EPS compared to a year ago:      0.0%     +
 - Expected annual SALES GROWTH RATE is:           11%      +
 - Expected annual EPS GROWTH RATE is:             5%
 - 5-year PROFIT ON SALES TREND is:               DOWN      -
           10-Year trend is:                      FLAT
 - 5-year EARNINGS ON INVESTED CAPITAL TREND is:  DOWN      -
           10-Year trend is:                      DOWN
 - Current PRICE/EARNINGS RATIO is:                8        +
 - Current PRICE/SALES RATIO is:                   0.61     +
 - PRICE in 5 years may increase by a factor of:  2.5       +
 - UPSIDE/DOWNSIDE RATIO is:                 4.8 to 1        +
 - Sum of expected YIELD plus PRICE GROWTH RATE:  23.0%     +
```

Figure 9-20   Printout of Summary Page from computer program to fill out the Stock Selection Guide.

```
                    3 - P R I C E - E A R N I N G S   H I S T O R Y

    PRESENT PRICE:      12  HIGH THIS YEAR:      13  LOW THIS YEAR:        8
    ----------------------------------------------------------------------------

                              EARNGS        PRICE         DVDND
                    PRICE       PER     EARNINGS RATIO      PER      %      % HIGH
          YEAR    HIGH   LOW   SHARE    HIGH     LOW       SHARE   PAYOUT   YIELD
    ----------------------------------------------------------------------------
           80      19     7    0.85     22.4     8.2       0.14    16.5%    2.0%
           81    14.1    6.1   0.74     19.1     8.2       0.15    20.3%    2.5%
           82     9.6    6.5   0.20     48.0    32.5       0.15    75.0%    2.3%
           83    13.5    7.9   0.37     36.5    21.4       0.15    40.5%    1.9%
           84    12.5    8.1   0.84     14.9     9.6       0.15    17.9%    1.9%

    ----------------------------------------------------------------------------
    TOTAL             35.6            140.8    80.0                170%
    AVERAGE            7              28.2     16.0                 34%
    ----------------------------------------------------------------------------
       AVERAGE PRICE EARNINGS RATIO:    22.1    CURRENT RATIO:       8



               4 - E V A L U A T I N G   R I S K  and  R E W A R D
                           (Over the Next Five Years)

    A - HIGH PRICE - NEXT FIVE YEARS:

       Ave Hi P-E of 28.2 x Est Hi EPS of $1.07 = Est Hi Price of:        $30
    ----------------------------------------------------------------------------
    B - LOW PRICE - NEXT FIVE YEARS:

       Ave Lo P-E of 16.0 x Est Lo EPS of $0.84 = Est Lo Price of:        $13
                            Avg Lo Price of last five years    =          $7
                            Recent severe market Lo Price       =          $6
                            Price dividend will support         =          $6

                                 Avg of above low prices        =          $8
                                      Selected low price        =          $8
    ----------------------------------------------------------------------------
    C - ZONING

       Est Hi Price of $30 less Est Lo Price of $8 = Range of:            $22
                                        1/3 of Range =                     $7

                       ZONING:      LOW     HIGH
                                   ---------------------
                                    $8      $15  (BUY RANGE)
                                    $15     $22  (MAYBE RANGE)
                                    $22     $29  (SELL RANGE)
                                   ---------------------


          ********************************************************
              Present Market Price of $12 is in the  BUY range
          ********************************************************

    ----------------------------------------------------------------------------
    D - UP-SIDE DOWN-SIDE RATIO (Potential Gain vs. Risk of Loss)

    Estimated Hi Price of $30 less Current Price of $12              **********
    ------------------------------------------------------------  =   4.8 to 1
       Current Price of $12 less Sel Low Price of $8                **********
```

Figure 9-21 Printout of Sections 3 and 4 from computer program to fill out the Stock Selection Guide.

which I specify in advance (and which I can change at any time), giving me a quick idea of how well I like this stock.

The program then invites me to view graphs of historical and projected sales and earnings-per-share performances, and to make changes to the projected growth rates, etc. Having done this, the program recalculates and shows me a new summary screen.

From this point, I'm free to make menu selections which allow me to do just about anything I might wish, from viewing any section of the Guide independently (see Figure 9-21), including graphs of all important data, to printing and saving the data from the Guide on a disk file. Having the data on disk allows me to call back the stock study weeks or months later to add new data, without redoing the whole thing.

The program is actually a Symphony template; that is, the user is required to have Symphony (a popular but relatively expensive integrated "spreadsheet" program) and lots of memory. I use my template on an IBM-compatible MS–DOS computer with a Hercules high resolution graphics board. A high resolution board is desirable, but is not an absolute requirement. A standard IBM color graphics board will work, or so I'm told.

The company which produces it will soon have two other versions, one for Lotus 123 and another for BASIC, which should run on any IBM-compatible computer with graphics capability and requiring considerably less memory. None of the programs is expensive.

A nice touch the company is working on will allow the user to access the data needed by the Guide directly from an on-line database. This will save some trips to the library, but it does mean that the computer has to have an appropriate modem so it can communicate with the database over the telephone line.

The company that produces these programs will supply more information and sample printouts on request. Send stamped, self-addressed business envelope to Criterion House, P.O. Box 4144, Foster City, California, 94404.

Adding 10
Judgment to Analysis

Whether you use a computer or not, you must always remember that the Stock Selection Guide, useful though it is, is just that: a guide. You must supply the judgment. By themselves, numbers in boxes will not provide the necessary understanding of a company's prospects. Even though the stock evaluates to a "Buy" on the Guide, you shouldn't feel that your work is finished and the decision automatic. To add judgment, go through your completed Guide now, looking closely at all the words, lines, and numbers you've added.

CAPITALIZATION

By filling in the top of side one of the Stock Selection Guide, you have already learned something about the company which may be useful in your evaluation. You know how many shares of common and preferred stock exist (outstanding shares) and how many the company is allowed to issue in the future (authorized shares). These are important facts. For instance, in some situations you may want companies with large numbers of shares outstanding, while in other situations you may prefer companies with smaller amounts of outstanding shares. If you know that a company has a large number of shares authorized, you're aware of the possibility that at

106

some point in the future those shares might be issued and the value of your present shares might as a result be diluted; that is, the same amount of net income would then be spread over a larger number of shares, so that the Earnings Per Share is automatically lowered.

Debt

The long-term debt of a company may be significant during times of economic problems. Does it seem too high in relation to earnings? When interest rates are high, companies with low (or no) debt are at an advantage.

RECENT QUARTERLY FIGURES

Look at the percentage changes in sales and earnings per share for the latest quarter. Are they up or down? Even though you've completed the entire Guide for RPM, Inc., it's possible that for some other company under analysis you might abandon study of the stock at this point. If the current percentage change is negative for sales or earnings or both, you might decide the company isn't growing and isn't suitable.

However, negative figures here aren't necessarily a reason to drop the stock. There may be good reasons why sales or earnings for the current quarter are down. Read the fine print on the Value Line or Standard & Poor's sheet from which you gained your information. Perhaps the entire economy is suffering from a recession, or that particular industry is having a temporary decline. The company may have had a nonrecurring expense which caused earnings to dip temporarily.

VISUAL ANALYSIS

Your red and blue lines, trend lines, and price bars give you a picture of the history of the company and a "guesstimate" of its future. In the case of RPM, the lines were relatively straight, but in some companies they may zigzag up and down. If sales for the last few years are all headed down and the information you read indicates the company's fortunes are waning, you might stop, throw away the sheet, and turn to the next company on your list.

At any time during the Stock Selection Guide preparation, if you're not satisfied with the company's record, for any logical reason, throw it out and go on to another. Your time is valuable and you shouldn't waste it on unlikely candidates. To repeat, the average investment club member spends only a couple of hours per month on stock analysis. If you find yourself spending a great deal more, either you're wasting your time on hopeless stocks or other members are not doing their fair share of the work.

In order to fill out the second page of the Guide, you had to draw a trend line for earnings and then use that figure to estimate a possible high five years into the future. In the case of RPM, you used the trend line charted from the previous ten-year earnings record. But suppose you decided that 12 percent was too conservative for this company? That since sales are growing at 16 percent a year, earnings might well grow at about the same rate for the next five years? In that case you would draw an adjusted trend line, such as the one you'll see in Figure 10-1, and use the new estimated earnings in your calculations.

Similarly, you might find a company whose earnings are unrealistically high. If the trend line is exceptionally steep, indicating a 40 to 50 percent annual growth rate, can you expect it to continue at that rate in the future? Perhaps the trend has been exaggerated by a few unusually high years. Remember in previous chapters you learned to look for a growth rate of 8 to 10 percent for large established companies, and 10 to 15 percent for smaller companies. Isn't a rate of 40 to 50 percent unsustainable for long periods?

I judge that it is and I would draw a new dotted trend line, from 1984 to 1989, at a lower rate, say 15 to 20 percent. An example is given in Figure 10-2. For help in this kind of analysis, look at future estimates given by Value Line and other services. Stock market experts are very happy with a 15 percent annual growth rate. And a 20 percent rate, one that results in a stock's value doubling in four years, is very difficult to sustain.

Suppose the trend line shows a growth rate of 5 percent or less? Since you're looking for a minimum growth of 8 percent, you might decide to abandon the company at this time. However, suppose that on completion of the Stock Selection Guide the stock met all other criteria and its expected average yield is 9 percent or more. This might be true of utility stocks for example. You might consider such a stock because its total return (growth plus yield) is your hoped-for 14 percent per year. You should probably not keep many such stocks in your portfolio, however. The best results are usually achieved by clubs with more diversification, including a considerable percentage of high-growth companies.

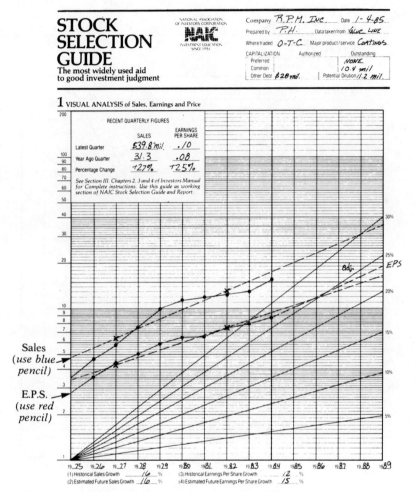

STOCK SELECTION GUIDE
The most widely used aid
to good investment judgment

NATIONAL ASSOCIATION OF INVESTORS CORPORATION
NAIC
INVESTMENT EDUCATION SINCE 1951

Company *R.P.M. Inc.* Date *1-4-85*
Prepared by *P.H.* Data taken from *Value Line*
Where traded *O-T-C* Major product/service *Coatings*

CAPITALIZATION   Authorized   Outstanding
Preferred   *NONE*
Common   *10.4 mil*
Other Debt *$28 mil.*   Potential Dilution *1.2 mil.*

1 VISUAL ANALYSIS of Sales, Earnings and Price

RECENT QUARTERLY FIGURES

	SALES	EARNINGS PER SHARE
Latest Quarter	*539.8 mil*	*.10*
Year Ago Quarter	*31.3*	*.08*
Percentage Change	*+27%*	*+25%*

See Section III. Chapters 2, 3 and 4 of Investors Manual for Complete instructions. Use this guide as working section of NAIC Stock Selection Guide and Report.

Sales
(use blue
pencil)

E.P.S.
(use red
pencil)

(1) Historical Sales Growth *16* %   (3) Historical Earnings Per Share Growth *12* %
(2) Estimated Future Sales Growth *16* %   (4) Estimated Future Earnings Per Share Growth *15* %

Figure 10-1   Side one of Stock Selection Guide for RPM, Inc., showing adjusted Earnings Trend Line.

You learn valuable facts about the company by looking at the growth in sales compared with the rate of growth in earnings. If sales are up 20 percent but earnings only 10 percent, profit margins (the ability to turn sales into earnings by, for example, keeping expenses in line) are slipping and it would seem something is wrong. On the other hand, earnings growing faster than sales may mean great efficiency. Large differences between these two figures should certainly cause you to do further research,

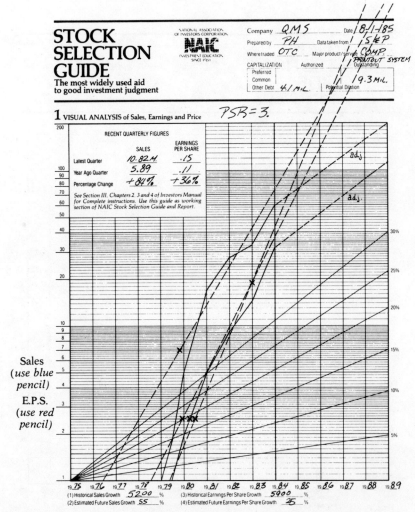

STOCK SELECTION GUIDE

NATIONAL ASSOCIATION OF INVESTORS CORPORATION

NAIC

INVESTMENT EDUCATION SINCE 1951

The most widely used aid to good investment judgment

Company *QMS* Date *8-1-85*

Prepared by *PH* Data taken from *S&P*

Where traded *OTC* Major product/service *COMP. PRINTOUT SYSTEM*

CAPITALIZATION Authorized Outstanding

Preferred

Common *19.3 Mil.*

Other Debt *4.1 Mil.* Potential Dilution

1 VISUAL ANALYSIS of Sales, Earnings and Price *PSR = 3.*

RECENT QUARTERLY FIGURES

	SALES	EARNINGS PER SHARE
Latest Quarter	*10.82 M.*	*.15*
Year Ago Quarter	*5.89*	*.11*
Percentage Change	*+84%*	*+36%*

See Section III, Chapters 2, 3 and 4 of Investors Manual for Complete instructions. Use this guide as working section of NAIC Stock Selection Guide and Report.

Sales (*use blue pencil*)

E.P.S. (*use red pencil*)

(1) Historical Sales Growth *52.00* % (3) Historical Earnings Per Share Growth *59.00* %

(2) Estimated Future Sales Growth *55* % (4) Estimated Future Earnings Per Share Growth *25* %

Figure 10-2 Side one of Stock Selection Guide for QMS, showing exceptionally high Sales and Earnings Trend Lines.

as generally the two figures remain nearly equal over the long run.

Finally, like soldiers marching across the page, the black vertical lines you drew to indicate stock prices over the past ten years show at a glance the price picture in relation to the sales and earnings figures. Those lines give you another opportunity to apply judgment. The Visual Analysis might show that the price of a certain stock has been much higher in the past and that the company's sales and earnings are growing at acceptable rates; judgment sug-gests that there is an opportunity for the price of the stock to rise to its former level.

EVALUATING MANAGEMENT

Turning to side two of the Guide (Figure 9-14), we see that for RPM both the Pre-Tax Profit on Sales and the Percent Earned on Invested Capital have been consistent. Profit margins have already been discussed. They should be steady or increasing slowly, but a slight downtrend is no great cause for alarm. Some companies show pre-tax profits of 10 percent, but often this depends on the industry. Food chains, for example, have much lower rates.

The Percent Earned on Invested Capital figure in **B** indicates how well the company is using the money which has been invested in it. Some analysts look for a consistent 16 to 17 percent, but such a company may not be easy to find. At any rate, the percentage should be higher than fixed income rates, such as those for Trea-sury bills.

The two figures from Section **2** tell you how this particular business is doing, especially in relation to other companies in the same industry. Some types of business traditionally return higher or lower amounts, so industry conditions must be taken into account for proper analysis.

PRICE/EARNINGS HISTORY

Price/Earnings (or P/E) ratios are found by dividing the per-share price of the stock by its per-share earnings for that year. If the current price of a stock is $50.00 and its earnings are $2.50, the P/E ratio is 20. With a share price of $25.00, the P/E ratio would be 10. This figure tells you how much investors have been willing to pay for those earnings.

At this point, if you judge the current Price-Earnings Ratio to be too high, you might abandon your study of this particular stock. Some investors feel that 10 is a good number; they hesitate to buy a stock with a higher P/E ratio. During the "go-go" years of the sixties when stock prices were accelerating rapidly and there seemed no end in sight, investors paid as much as sixty times earnings for some companies.

Some investment clubs make rules about how high the P/E

ratio should be, and the N.A.I.C. suggests avoiding a stock if the P/E Ratio is higher than the average of the past five years. In the case of RPM, the current and five-year-average P/E ratios are equal, but if the highest average P/E ratio for the last five years had been 15 and the ratio currently stood at 18, you'd probably feel the stock is over-priced. Even if the current P/E ratio is above just the *average* of both the high and low averages, it may be too high and not suitable for your portfolio.

Kenneth Janke, President of N.A.I.C. Incorporated, in a talk to the San Francisco Bay Area Council in August 1985, offered the "Rule of 20" for considering P/E ratios. It has been his observation that they reflect the rate of inflation. In the sixties, when inflation was 3 percent, P/E ratios of the stocks making up the Standard & Poor's 500 Index averaged about 17 percent, or a total of inflation plus P/E ratios of 20. When inflation was 12 percent, Standard & Poor's 500 Index P/E ratios averaged 8 percent, again totalling 20. Today, with inflation running about 4 percent annually, a P/E ratio of 16 is not unrealistic, since that, too, would total 20.

If a company shows steadily rising sales and earnings over many years, its P/E ratio may be rising as well. In that case, a more accurate prediction of its future P/E might be gained by canceling out the two oldest (lowest) numbers and averaging the remaining three.

DIVIDENDS

Dividends are like interest on your money, and can be expressed as the Yield (see Figure 9-15, column H), the dividend-per-share amount divided by the per-share price of the stock. The Percent Payout, column G, which is found by dividing the dividend by the earnings and multiplying by 100, tells you how much of the earnings of the company are returned to the stockholder in the form of dividends (the balance being retained by the company for expansion or other legitimate reasons).

Some companies traditionally pay out large sums; others are more conservative. It's often argued that growth companies pay out a smaller percentage of earnings to shareholders so that they may finance internal growth. This will, it's hoped, result in stronger capital appreciation later. Most growth companies pay out less than 50 percent in dividends; for aggressive growth, you might look for companies which pay out less than 30 percent of their earnings in dividends. Some new, growing companies pay no dividends at all.

As you look at the figures you entered in Section **3**, watch for any unusually high or low numbers which could tend to distort the averages. Like Olympics judges, you may want to throw out the unusual high or low and average the rest. Doing this might affect the rest of your calculations on the Guide and result in a second, harder look at the company you're studying.

EVALUATING RISK AND REWARD

Look at Item **4–A**, (Figure 9-18), the high price the Guide forecast for this stock five years into the future. Is it at least double the current price, meeting your goal?

Item **4-B** requires listing some low prices, among them the "recent severe market low price." Some clubs interpret this to mean the lowest price of the last five years; others prefer to use the lowest price of the current year. Depending on which figure you use here, there could be a significant variation in the final forecast low price you select.

For example, in the case of RPM, if you use the $10 price (as was done in the sample) and average the four numbers under **B**, you end up with a forecast price of $9. On the other hand, if you use $5, your final price will be $8. Admittedly, in this particular case the difference is slight, but it can be wider in stocks with vastly different numbers. You might want to take a conservative approach and work out the Guide both ways, then choose the one that suits you.

By subtracting the forecast low from the forecast high and dividing by three, you set up "zones" between these extremes that gave a rough estimate of when to buy the stock. Ideally the current price of the stock should fall into the Buy zone, as does RPM in our example. If it falls into the Maybe zone, you might still consider a purchase because of other factors, or you might set it aside and look at it from time to time to see if the price has dropped into the Buy zone.

Many years ago, our club filled out a Stock Selection Guide on Tandy Corporation just after the stock had risen in price from $9 to $19 a share. Although $19 was still in the Buy zone, which went up to $36, some members felt that the sudden run-up could not be repeated and voted down the motion to buy. By the next club meeting, the price had risen to $31, which many members insisted certainly couldn't be duplicated. By the next month the price was $39, out of the Buy range, and no vote was taken.

But one member, who remained keen on the stock, gradually convinced others; when the price dipped to $35 she made the motion again and this time it passed. The stock subsequently split, rose again to about $42 a share, and spun off two other companies, Tandy Brands and Tandycrafts, one of which spun off another company, Stafford-Lowdon. At one point half our portfolio consisted of the four stocks we owned as a result of the one purchase of Tandy. When we sold Tandy we had more than doubled our investment in about three years. We also made a profit on the remaining companies when they were sold.

When a company "spins off" another company (usually one of its divisions or branches), it issues stock to its shareholders in proportion to the stock already owned by them. This, in effect, costs the shareholder nothing, although it's treated on the books as a "stock dividend," and the issuing company suggests a price which is used as the basis of determining gain or loss and for income tax purposes.

As a footnote to this story, a few years later we again investigated Tandy Corporation, determined it was again in our Buy range, bought it, and enjoyed further profits.

By subtracting the current price from the high forecast price, and the forecast low price from the current price, then dividing the first difference by the second, you arrive at a figure which measures your risk. In other words, you're asking, "What are my chances the stock price will increase to my forecast high versus my chances it will drop to my forecast low?"

Before you make your bet (by buying the stock at the current price) you want to be sure this ratio is at least 3 to 1 in your favor. It's easy to see that the closer the current price is to the forecast low, the higher this number, and the better your timing skills.

Another way of interpreting this figure is that the price doesn't have far to fall to be at the bottom, so you won't lose much if it drops, but there's plenty of room to increase and you're therefore more likely to have big profits if the price rises to your expected high.

FIVE-YEAR POTENTIAL

In the sample (Figure 9-19), the current yield is 3.5 percent and the five-year average yield is also 3.5 percent. As you've already learned, the dividend can be helpful in increasing your total portfolio value. By adding the yield of 3.5 percent to the expected price increase of 100 percent, you see the possibility that you'll enjoy a total return of 103.5 percent on your investment.

As a final step, staple to the back of the Stock Selection Guide any reference information you have about the company, such as a brokerage house report or magazine article.

Having completed Guides on all the companies you wished to study (or else eliminated them all!), you'll have formed some opinions by now. Some stocks will appeal to you more than others. Generally, one will appear to be "best." Some members throw out all but the best and present this one to their club at the next meeting. Others bring all of them for discussion by the members. Another member may know of developments within a company that make it more or less desirable than its Stock Selection Guide would indicate.

At the meeting, member-prepared Stock Selection Guides will be passed around, examined, and discussed. A Stock Comparison Guide (available from the N.A.I.C.) might be filled out, making it easier for members to determine which of several choices is their best at this time (see Figure 10-3.) At this point a vote may be taken. If a stock you especially admire is not purchased at that time, hold onto your Guide, update it, and bring them back to the next meeting.

If you've been assigned an industry or have studied several stocks, fill out a Comparison Guide yourself and bring it to the meeting along with the Stock Selection Guides on all the companies you studied.

When a stock is purchased, a club member may be required to keep track of it from then until it's sold. For this purpose, a Portfolio Management Guide from the N.A.I.C. (see Figure 10-4) will show you a systematic way to keep track of the price, earnings, and price/earnings ratio of the stock. In some clubs the Portfolio Management Guide is discussed at every meeting.

Newer clubs, especially those with little money to invest at one time, may buy only a few shares at first and gradually add to their holdings of that stock over the next few months, provided the price remains in their Buy zone. This, as we've discussed earlier, is known as "dollar-cost averaging" and can be very beneficial. If the price is rising as you buy additional shares, it's also known as "averaging up."

We've discussed averaging down, which seems to be attractive to many clubs but can lead to trouble. If you've purchased a stock at $20 and it drops to $10, you consider it a bargain, and most

STOCK COMPARISON GUIDE

NATIONAL ASSOCIATION
OF INVESTORS CORPORATION

NAIC

INVESTMENT EDUCATION
SINCE 1951

Prepared by _____

Date _____

See Section III, Chapter 5 of the Investors Manual for complete instructions.

NAME OF COMPANY

GROWTH COMPARISON (From Section 1 of N.A.I.C. Stock Selection Guide)					
(1) Historical % of Sales Growth					
(2) Projected % of Sales Growth					
(3) Historical % of Earnings Per Share Growth					
(4) Projected % of Earnings Per Share Growth					

MANAGEMENT COMPARISONS (From Sec. 2 of N.A.I.C. Stock Selection Guide)

(5) % Profit Margin Before Taxes (Average for last 5 years)	(2A) Trend					
(6) % Earned on Invested Capital (Average for last 5 years)	(2B) Trend					
(7) % of Common Owned by Management						

PRICE COMPARISONS (See Section 3, N.A.I.C. Stock Selection Guide)

(8) Estimated Total Earnings Per Share For Next Five Years							
(9) Price Range Over Last 5 Years	High (3A) Low (3B)						
(10) Present Price							
Price Earnings Ratio Range Last 5 Years	(11) Highest	(3D)					
	(12) Average High	(3D7)					
	(13) Average	(3-8)					
	(14) Average Low	(3E7)					
	(15) Lowest	(3E)					
(16) Current Price Earnings Ratio	(3-9)						
Estimated Price Zones	(17) Lower – Buy	(4C2)					
	(18) Middle – Maybe	(4C3)					
	(19) Upper – Sell	(4C4)					
(20) Present Price Range	(4C5)						
(21) Upside Downside Ratio	(4D)						
(22) Current Yield	(5A)						
(23) Combined Estimated Yield							

OTHER COMPARISONS

(24) Number of Common Shares Outstanding						
(25) Potential Dilution from Debentures, Warrants, Options						
(26) Percent Payout	(3G7)					
(27)						
(28)						
(29) Date of Source Material						
(30) Where Traded						

© 1983. National Association of Investors Corporation; 1515 E. Eleven Mile Road, Royal Oak, MI 48067

Figure 10-3   Sample of N.A.I.C. Stock Comparison Guide.

people find bargains hard to resist. Unfortunately, the record shows that in many cases the stock doesn't go up from there; it goes further down. Be very sure, when you average down, that the

NAIC
INVESTMENT
EDUCATION
EST.
1951

THE NATIONAL ASSOCIATION OF INVESTMENT CLUBS
PORTFOLIO MANAGEMENT GUIDE
SEE CHAPTER IV-I OF THE INVESTMENT CLUB MANUAL FOR INSTRUCTIONS ON USE OF THIS GUIDE!

STOCK: _____ ANALYST: _____

I PRICE EARNINGS ZONES   Refer to 2A, columns D and E, line 7, of your Stock Selection Guide study of this company for the information in columns 2 and 3 below.

1	2	3	4	5	6
YEAR	Average Price Earnings Ratios for Previous Five Years		Sum of Cols. 2 and 3	Column 4 Divided by 2	Column 5 Multiplied by 1½
	High	Low		Low P/E Guide Line	High P/E Guide Line

II PRICE ZONES   See Section 2B4 of Stock Selection Guide. 1 below is top of Buy Zone. 2 below is bottom of Sell Zone

YEAR	1. Consider Buying Below	2. Consider Selling Above

III CUMULATIVE EARNINGS AND CURRENT PRICE-EARNINGS RATIO COMPUTATIONS

1	2	3	4	5	6	7	8	9	10	11	12
3 Months Ending	Earnings per Share	Total Earnings for last 4 Quarters	Date	Price	P/E Ratio at Time of Meeting	Date	Price	P/E Ratio at Time of Meeting	Date	Price	P/E Ratio at Time of Meeting

Figure 10-4   Sample of N.A.I.C. Portfolio Management Guide.

fundamentals of the company are still good. Are its sales and earnings increasing? Is the company well managed, with acceptable profit margins and return on equity? If on the other hand, earnings have slipped or there is other bad news about the company, you'd be better advised to cut your losses quickly rather than buy more just because it looks cheap.

Averaging up can be profitable. If a stock is performing well, why not buy more? As long as the stock's price remains in the Buy range, it's a better prospect than another company, one whose stock you *hope* will go up. When new earnings reports appear, update your Stock Selection Guide; the Buy range may expand, indicating that the stock may be profitably purchased at an even higher price.

At least two clubs with which I'm familiar have achieved impressive results with this strategy. Some clubs, however, prefer to buy a different stock every month and not study a past purchase unless something significant occurs or until their once-a-year evaluation of all stocks in the portfolio.

For the individual investor, completion of the Stock Selection Guide should lead to a decision to buy or not to buy that stock. You don't have to get anyone else to agree with you and wait for a favorable vote. If you have many suitable stocks, save the Guides of those you don't purchase immediately and update them for consideration at a later date.

OTHER ANALYSIS TOOLS

Our club purchases an *Investor's Manual* for every member, and we have reordered them from time to time when the *Manual* has been significantly updated. An individual investor might want to own the *Manual* whether he or she belongs to the N.A.I.C. or not, because it's filled with investment club advice and many helpful articles on stock analysis.

The Stock Check List and Report, which are additional forms that the N.A.I.C. offers, were helpful when we began, although we no longer use them. Beginning clubs or individual investors may want to look these over to see if they can be useful.

We fill out a Stock Selection Guide before purchasing any stock and we have a poster-size version (available from the N.A.I.C.) for teaching new members and reminding older ones of how to fill them out. We make occasional use of the Stock Comparison Guide (Figure 10-3) and this too can be purchased in a large version. We also have a Portfolio Management Guide (Figure 10-4) for each stock. Individual investors are advised to purchase and use the Stock Selection Guide and to consider these other forms.

The N.A.I.C. Stock Study Course was not available when we

began, but I recommend it for new clubs. It can, perhaps, be even more helpful for individual investors, as they have no one with whom to discuss investing.

The N.A.I.C. also provides a form entitled Portfolio Evaluation Review Technique (PERT) on which investors enter information about the stocks they own to evaluate past performance and future prospects. Our club has not used this method, so I can't comment on its usefulness. Since our club has a "stock watcher," we leave it to this person to calculate and keep us informed of changes in price, earnings, P/E ratio, and any other facts about the company or its stock that seem pertinent. In addition, once a year we fill out a new Stock Selection Guide on the company to make a buy, hold, or sell decision. But an individual investor must be his or her own stock watcher at all times, and for that person PERT may be helpful. The *Manual* describes this technique in detail.

Before leaving this chapter, I must mention some aspects of evaluating stock that are not a part of the Stock Selection Guide or the N.A.I.C.'s evaluation. Some stock market experts think these aspects are important and, especially where you need to make a choice between several good companies, they may help in your decision.

"Book value" is found by subtracting total liabilities from total assets and dividing the difference by the number of shares outstanding. It can be found, already calculated, on both Value Line and Standard & Poor's reports, and represents the underlying value of the company. The book value is an indication of how much the stockholder would receive for each share owned if the company were dissolved and its assets, after all debts were paid, were distributed to the stockholders.

The stocks of most good companies rarely sell at or below book value except in severe bear markets. If you find a company whose stock price is close to book value, it may be a great bargain. Don't use book value as your sole analysis unless you become expert at analyzing annual reports, because it is a figure often misunderstood. For example, a company may own land which is listed on its books at the purchase price, which may be far below the land's current value. On the other hand, a company may show assets that prove to be almost worthless in actual liquidation (for instance, a bank might have uncollectible loans outstanding). The trend of book value (preferably up) is probably more important than the dollar amount.

Some analysts steer clear of companies with large amounts of authorized but unissued shares, because (as I explained earlier) if those shares are issued some time in the future, the value of the shares then outstanding could be lowered. Other analysts refuse to buy the common stock of companies authorized to sell preferred. Because preferred shareholders receive assets before common shareholders in the case of company failure and liquidation, such an investment seems less secure to these analysts.

Another possible way to determine the safety of an investment is to look at the company's financial base. First, current assets versus current liabilities should have a ratio of better than 1 to 1, preferably 1.5 or 2 to 1. These figures can be found in the annual report of the company. Second, the trend of working capital (working capital is the difference between current assets and current liabilities) ought to be increasing. Third, the ratio of debt to equity should be low. Divide the long-term debt by the total capitalization of the company. Since less debt is considered to give a company stability and flexibility, the lower the debt-equity ratio, the better this company will look to many analysts. Some analysts want no long-term debt at all; others will tolerate up to 30 percent of total capitalization.

Some analysts try to choose companies which are relatively free from government regulation, or those with a small or nonunion labor force, feeling that management will have more control over the destiny of the company.

Still others prefer to buy stocks of companies which have less than 10 percent of their outstanding stock in the hands of institutions. (Standard & Poor's report and other similar reports list this information.) As I explained earlier, institutions must invest very large sums and their buying and selling could cause excessive price swings.

"Insider" buying or selling influences some investors. For example, when corporate officers of a company are heavy buyers of their own stock, the stock's price often rises significantly in the next twelve months. Conversely, heavy insider selling sometimes causes price declines. Insiders must report their transactions, so this factor can be studied. One such report is entitled "The Insiders" and may be purchased from the Institute for Econometric Research in Ft. Lauderdale, Florida.

Another analysis tool, popularized in 1984 by Kenneth L. Fisher in his book *Super Stocks*, is the price/sales ratio, or PSR. This is determined by dividing the stock's total market value by the company's total revenues, or (it's the same thing) the stock price by the per-share revenues.

For example, if a company has total sales of $100 million and 5 million shares of stock outstanding, dividing the $100 million by 5 million gives us a figure of $20, which is the amount of sales per share. Should the price of the stock be $40, its price/sales ratio would be 2.0 ($40 divided by $20). A per-share price of $20 gives a PSR of 1. Value Line provides a shortcut to this computation by giving the revenues-per-share figure; merely divide this by the current price.

What do these numbers mean? We've already discussed the recommendations that the price-earnings ratio of a stock be no higher than its five-year-average P/E ratio and that you should consider selling a stock whose P/E ratio is more than twice that number. These ratios generally run from 5 to 30, although, as you've seen, outrageous numbers sometimes show up. With PSRs, the numbers to look for are 1 or less, and you consider selling a stock whose PSR has soared to 3.

The value of the PSR lies in the fact that sometimes price/earnings ratios are meaningless. A new company may have few earnings but outstanding potential in terms of sales. Sometimes a price/earnings ratio may be reasonable, yet sales are slipping and the stock price is sure to follow. Remember too that earnings are an after-the-fact number; by the time sales have been translated into earnings, savvy investors may have already bid up the shares, preventing your acquiring a bargain.

Whether you use any of these additional stock analysis theories will depend on your perception of their usefulness. Practice may really be the only way to evaluate them; and perhaps not even then—a phenomenon which may be explained in the next chapter.

Market Timing 11

WHAT MOVES THE MARKET?

Sometimes stock market action seems completely irrational. The stocks of stable, well-established companies with rising earnings, high book value, and no long-term debt, which would seem to be sure winners, will sometimes stay flat or even decline; whereas those of companies with falling earnings or no earnings at all may rise in price. It can be argued that in the long run quality will determine price, but the short run can be very frustrating when you're holding a stock that declines for months in spite of its superlative credentials.

The rationale for such market behavior is usually "The market doesn't value this," or (in the case of a near-bankrupt company showing rising stock prices) "The market is ignoring the signs," or "The market has already discounted it." Just who is this "market" that makes such strange evaluations?

The "market" can be described as the sum total of all the individuals, brokers, specialists, mutual funds, and institutions who buy or sell stock on any given day. Their aims are obviously very different. One individual may take advantage of a hot tip by his barber; a broker may sell stock today to pay an offspring's college tuition next week; the specialists must buy or sell to conduct an orderly market; a mutual fund may sell because it has had a large number of withdrawals this month and needs cash; and the institution may buy a particular stock because its research department turned in a glowing report on it.

One would think that, because of these random variations, it's impossible ever to predict future stock prices and make a profit on investing—luck must be in charge. The fact is, however, that despite the disparate reasons for buying and selling, individuals and institutions alike do buy or sell *en masse* most of the time. You've heard of "bull" markets and "bear" markets? Well, a bull market is when most investors buy and prices rise, and a bear market is when most sell and prices decline.

CYCLES

It's common knowledge that these bull and bear phases follow one another in cycles. When charted (using the Dow Jones Industrial Average, for example) as far back as the nineteenth century, these phases seem to follow each other in 4½ year cycles. In more recent years, the cycles appear to have shortened to about four years.

This is not exact; you can't predict the day (or even the month) a bear market will end. Sometimes a bottom will occur forty-five months after the last bottom, sometimes it will take sixty; but over the years the cycle seems to average fifty-four months. In Figure 11-1, which is a chart showing several stock market averages for the past thirty-six years, the Dow Jones Industrial Average, which is at the top of the chart, shows these dips quite plainly. I've marked the years in which the lows occur, and as you can see, they come approximately every four years. Some of the cycle bottoms have been relatively shallow. The decline in 1953 is an example of a mere dip in an otherwise constantly ascending line, which represents the long bull market that began after World War II and continued through the sixties.

Shortly after our club started, I read how, starting with $10,000, you could make a million dollars in the stock market in less than two years by taking advantage of cycles in stock prices. The book was written in 1971 and I read it in 1973. When the author showed a long-term chart of the Dow Jones Industrial Average indicating its 4½ year cycles, I was interested, and projected that the bottom of the next bear market would occur in December 1974. That one, at least, came right on schedule. The theory goes on to predict nine-year (two 4½ year) cycles and many shorter ones.

Our club members were very naive between 1972 and 1974,

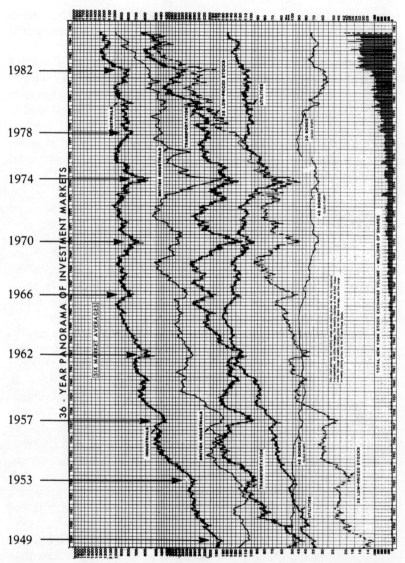

Figure 11-1   Securities Research chart of popular stock averages, indicating Bear Market Lows for past 36 years.

not realizing that our losses were due to the bear market rather than to our personal (collective) stupidity; but our continuing study convinced us that there is a way to tell when the entire market will rise or when it's likely to fall, based on factors discussed in such sources as the financial pages of the newspapers, especially *Barron's* and in magazines such as *Money, Fortune, Time, Forbes,* etc.

There are many cycle theories to account for the movement of stock prices. One theory is that the presidential election, occurring every four years, has something to do with the gradual shortening of the 4½ year cycle to four. As the federal government plays an ever-greater role in the economy (by fixing interest rates, for instance), such a theory makes some sense.

The Kondratieff wave cycle theory, born during the twenties, describes market movements in terms of fifty- to sixty-year waves (about the then-average life expectancy). Kondratieff was a Russian economist assigned to predict the collapse of American capitalism, but he predicted instead that the cycles would enable the system to continue. He was banished to Siberia.

There is also an Elliot wave cycle theory, and another theory which says you can determine a bull or bear market by the height of women's skirts!

INTEREST RATES

There is no question in most minds today that when interest rates go up the stock market will go down. This makes perfect sense. People have less reason to risk their money in the stock market when they can earn a guaranteed — and often insured — 10 to 20 percent on their funds by leaving them in a bank, savings and loan institution, or money market fund. The investment club, as well as the individual investor, should do no less.

At any given time investors should have most of their funds in those investments which will bring about the greatest return. When interest rates are high, you should move out of stocks. When interest rates drop, and it's again possible to buy stocks yielding reasonable rates of return and offering the hope of capital appreciation, the funds can be moved from such fixed-rate instruments and returned to the stock market.

That this is true is illustrated perfectly by what happened between 1979 and 1982. When money market rates were 18 percent, it was foolish to invest widely in the stock market and the Dow Jones Industrial Average showed it, hovering between 780 and 880 for an entire year. But in August 1982, with inflation reduced to 5 percent, the discount rate down to 8.5 percent, and interest rates dropping to about 10 percent, the market took off like the proverbial rocket, toppling all old records. The Dow Jones Industrial Average soared to 1270 within a year.

TO BUY OR TO HOLD

The N.A.I.C.'s first rule is to buy regularly, regardless of whether we think the market is going up or down; the organization also warns against trying to second-guess the market. Despite the warning, we've seen that during periods of high interest rates we can expect a bear market.

In *Better Investing* in October 1983, Charles S. Ricker, Chartered Financial Analyst of Sigma Management Services, wrote, "Higher interest rates, of course, imply lower security prices and lower, interest rates imply higher security prices. According to an old Wall Street cliche, 'The Federal Reserve writes the market letter for Wall Street.'"

An individual investor's or investment club's portfolio can benefit from having a good portion of cash in a savings account during periods of high interest rates and low stock prices. Since you're looking for 14.4 percent annual growth, why shouldn't you get an insured 14 to 18 percent on your money when it's offered, rather than watch the value of your stocks decline as much as 50 percent, which is what happened to even the best blue chip stocks during the periods 1972–1974 and 1976–1978.

To continue to hold stocks while they drop rapidly seems foolhardy to me, similar to holding on in 1929. The Dow Jones Industrial Average peaked at 381 that year and never went that high again until 1954, twenty-five years later!

Assume for a moment that it was possible to buy a share of the Dow Jones Industrial Average in 1929 for $381. Had you held on for twenty-five years, it would have again been worth $381 in 1954. But suppose you had sold it when it began dropping. Not being clairvoyant, you didn't know the market was going to fall so rapidly, but you had set a limit for a loss of, say, 15 percent, after which you would sell. Therefore you sold the hypothetical share at $324. And suppose you held this cash until 1932 when the market began to recover. The market bottomed out at $41, but since you weren't clairvoyant you didn't buy then, but waited until it moved up 15 percent to $47. Your $324 could now buy 6.89 shares of the Dow Jones Industrial Average, and by 1954 these shares were worth $2,626.

Thus, in the first case you earned zero and in the second you earned almost 600 percent on your money.

Of course, it could be argued that had you held it, your share of stock would have earned dividends for you during those twenty-five years; but you might have put your $324 in a bank and earned interest until you bought back into the market; in that case you might have done even better. In addition, when you bought back in, you were able to buy more than six shares and thus had six times the dividends from 1933 to 1954. That would more than compensate for the brokers' commissions on your trades.

Although you can't buy a share in the Dow Jones Industrial Average, you can buy shares in the thirty stocks that go to make up this average and the same logic applies. (You can now buy Index futures, but you must look elsewhere for information on those, as I'm sticking to common stocks in this book.) International Business Machines (IBM), one of the stocks that makes up that average, dropped from over $600 a share in 1972 to under $200 in 1974. Had you sold your shares near the top and bought back at the bottom, you could have tripled your investment. Even selling at 15 percent off the top and bottom would have meant more than doubling your investment.

As I've just shown, a buy and hold policy is not always the most prudent. There are times when even the best company's stock should be sold. It may be bought back at a later time or it may not, as circumstances dictate.

Another book I ran across a few years ago proposed the theory that there are stocks, which, if you hold them long enough, would not only double, but increase in value 100 times! The author listed 100 stocks which had done this over the past eighty years. A few of these stocks grew 100 times in as little as five years; but most required far longer.

On the surface this seems like good support for the buy and hold theory, but let's give it more thought. There are literally thousands of companies to choose from, a staggering number of choices. Out of so many, finding the one or two stocks today that will eventually appreciate 100 times is comparable to looking for the proverbial needle in a haystack. The odds for your finding even one are dismal.

Furthermore, every day of every one of those eighty years, you'll be faced with the decision of whether to buy, hold, or sell. The author of the book didn't give a clue as to how to determine which stocks to buy and hold. He simply found them the easy way, by hindsight and a computer program!

During the sixties there was a Wall Street truism that went, "Never sell IBM," but the fact is that a buy and hold policy in IBM would not have been as profitable as a buy and sell and buy back approach, as you've already seen.

Of course, the key to such success is in knowing when the turnarounds will occur. This is where the timing of cycles comes in.

INDICATORS

Cycles are seldom apparent until after the movement has occurred, but certain "indicators" of cycles do exist. Indicators are particular statistics about the stock market which are believed to show the direction—up or down—that prices as a whole (as shown by such averages as the Dow Jones Industrial Average or the Standard & Poor's 500 Index or the New York Stock Exchange Composite) will take.

These indicators are numerous, and you may have heard of some of them. There are money indicators such as the discount rate, the margin rate, and the federal funds rate. If you follow these indicators and they tell you that money is tight, it may be a clue to you that a bear market is in progress or coming soon. It's no secret that interest rates alone seem to control much of the market movement.

There are indicators of the price direction of many stocks, such as moving averages, the advance-decline line (see the Glossary for definitions), and the number of stocks making new highs and lows, as reported in the *Wall Street Journal* or *Barrons*. These might indicate to you that the market is "overbought" (nearing or at the top of a bull phase) or that it's "oversold" nearing or at the bottom of a bear phase).

There are odd-lot indicators, specialists' indicators, short-selling indicators, and many, many more. Some analysts swear by certain indicators and feel that paying attention to such pointers improves their stock market performance. Consult *A Strategy of Daily Stock Market Timing for Maximum Profit* by Joseph E. Granville, or *Stock Market Logic* by Norman Fosback to learn more about such indicators.

One of the members of my club follows six indicators, most of them having to do with money rates, because we feel that they influence the direction of the market. We also watch the Dow Jones Utilities Average, as we feel that is an indication of investment strength. In addition, we believe that when the yield on the thirty stocks which make up the Dow Jones Industrial Average is 3 percent or more, the outlook is bullish; if under 3 percent, it's bearish. We don't arbitrarily sell our stocks if these indicators turn bearish; we do consider the indicators, however, when our stocks fail to perform adequately. Our selling rules are listed in Chapter 12.

Entire schools of investing theory have sprung up because of these and other market phenomena. As for almost every other aspect of the stock market, there are books on the subject of stock market indicators; check your library if you want to know more about them.

TECHNICAL ANALYSIS

"Why," some ask, "should we try to understand the motives of different investors? Why not simply observe their collective action — see whether the stock price goes up or down — and act accordingly?"

This approach is called "technical analysis" as opposed to "fundamental analysis," which you learned about in earlier chapters. You looked at the company's prospects — its fundamentals — to determine if the price might rise.

But "technicians" say that such study is a waste of time. Good companies often go unrewarded for years (as do good people!), while lesser companies enjoy popularity. For example, in 1969, a bull market year, the stock of a computer maker with no sales (let alone earnings) sold for $19 a share. A leasing firm's stock sold at $45 in spite of no earnings. A small, new company had a P/E ratio of 290!

Technicians believe that individual stocks, as well as the market as a whole, have cycles; that most stocks, when charted, will show the same four to four-and-a-half year cycles as the market; but that within *these* cycles are shorter cycles which can be used to mark buying and selling opportunities.

We all know that stock prices never march upward in a perfectly straight line: 10 today, 10¼ tomorrow, then 10½, 11, 11½, 12, and so on. Instead the movement is more variable: 10¼, 10, 10½, 11, 10½, 11, 11½, 11, 11½, 12. According to the technicians, these fluctuations are the net result of various minor cyclical components.

In one of the oldest cycle theories still being followed, the Dow Theory, these minor movements are called "ripples." Larger up and down movements are called "waves," and finally we have the greater "swings," which determine bull and bear markets.

So how do the technicians decide which stock to buy or sell?

They're not concerned with the type of company—in fact the chartists (as they are known) pay little attention to what the company does—but merely the movement of its stock price. They don't analyze the company's sales, earnings, or capitalization. They watch the price action and, often, the volume of shares traded each day.

The technical analyst draws lines, or circles and crosses, on a chart; by studying the appearance of these marks, he or she determines if a stock is in a position to be bought or sold.

There are two main types of charts which technicians use in their analyses. One is the common graph using vertical lines to represent the daily high and low of a stock's price (with perhaps a horizontal bar to indicate the closing price), just like the lines you drew on the front of the Stock Selection Guide to indicate the annual highs and lows (see Figure 11-2).

The other type is called a "point and figure" chart: a circle is made in an appropriate box when the stock price declines and an **x** when it advances. If the price does not change by a predetermined amount that day, no mark is made (see Figure 11-3).

By looking at these charts the analyst determines buy and sell points (or support and resistance levels) for the stock.

This is a gross simplification and you should read books on the subject if you're interested. Usually *Better Investing* carries an article on the point and figure type of stock chart and analysis in each issue; if you're a member of an investment club, you might wish to discuss this with other club members.

One investment club reported to me that in 1984 a member made a point and figure chart for Key Pharmaceuticals, a stock they were considering buying, and it indicated to them that the stock price could slip. Although they bought the stock at $16 a share, they entered a stop loss order with their broker at $14, the point where the chart showed a possible sell signal; sure enough, the price dropped and they sold out. The stock's price subsequently sank to less than $9, thereby justifying their precautions and turning them into charting enthusiasts.

I mention technical analysis because it can be used to good advantage, even with individuals or clubs which normally use fundamental analysis for buying stock. Most clubs with which I am acquainted, in fact, use fundamental analysis to determine which stocks to buy, and technical analysis to determine when to sell them. In other words, they pay attention to cycles.

Another theory of stock market analysis is called the "random walk theory." Whereas fundamental analysis insists you can predict

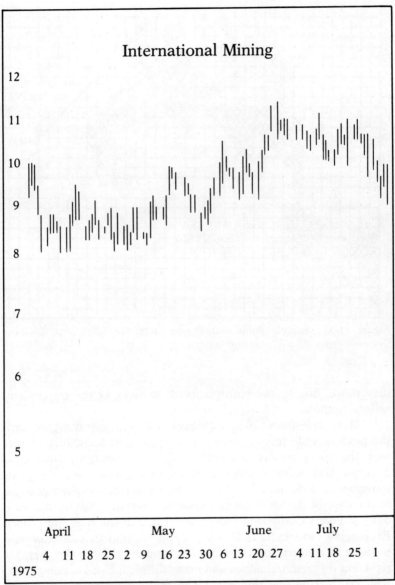

Figure 11-2   Daily Price Graph for International Mining Co.

the future price of a stock by studying the company's inner workings and technical analysis insists you can do so by studying its past price movements, the random walk theory says that both of these are wrong: there is simply no way to predict prices, because

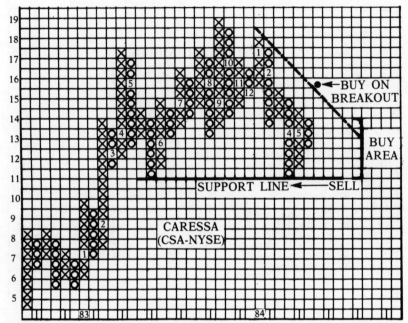

Figure 11-3 Sample Point and Figure Chart for Safeguard Business Systems, from *Better Investing* Magazine.

they move, due to the multiplicity of motives of the buyers and sellers, randomly.

Most investment club members will certainly disagree with the random walk theory, since they've produced handsome results over the years by fundamental analysis. Most technicians also disagree and point to their own successes. Since it's the price movements of the individual stocks that make up the averages—30 in the case of the Dow Jones Industrial Average, 500 in the Standard & Poor's Composite Index, and 1,600 in the New York Stock Exchange's Composite Index—it's apparent that these stocks tend to move in concert and therefore not randomly. Since the averages represent different industries and many different kinds of companies, why do they behave this way? The random walk theory doesn't account for cycles, yet we have seen that cycles certainly exist.

Our club generally buys on fundamental analysis and sells on either fundamental or technical. You could say that we pay attention to cycles when selling but not when buying. Since we have a constant inflow of new money, we try to put it to work in the market; but it stands to reason that when the top of a bull market is near (as indicated by technical analysis) there will be few companies whose fundamental statistics indicate a reasonable price is possible. When stocks have run up for a year or two, their prices are out of our Buy range. Therefore, we find ourselves doing little buying for technical as well as fundamental reasons.

One high-ranking investment club, which earned an average of more than 45 percent per year for sixteen years, reported that its procedures are as much technical as fundamental. Their portfolio consists of only six issues and all they do is vary the amount of their total investment in each one. For example, when a stock increases in price so that the club's investment in that stock reaches 25 percent of the club's total investment, some of it is sold, bringing that percentage down to 15 to 20. At the same time, if investment in a company drops to 10 percent of the club's total investment, they purchase additional stock to bring it's share of the total to 15 to 20 percent. Another top club, which has averaged more than a 30 percent increase over its three-and-a-half-year life, stated that it used analysis of bull and bear cycles to influence buy and sell decisions. A ten-year-old club whose 25 percent annual return has gained it recognition also used a system for judging bull and bear markets and some other stock market indicators. Still another ten-year-old club, which earned more than 19 percent per year, frankly admitted that it has a speculative bias, makes decisions based on analysis of cycles, and takes larger risks than the N.A.I.C. recommends.

As we discuss these numbers, it's helpful to remember that the average club reporting its results in 1982 showed gains of 5.87 percent over its lifetime. It would seem, therefore, that market timing bears some investigation and might play a significant role in improving investment results.

When to Sell 12

There are two parts to investing in the stock market: buying and selling. And although experts bombard us from all sides with advice on what to buy, no one tells us what to sell (or, rather, as this chapter has it, *when* to sell).

Money brings many psychological factors into play. In our society at least, money represents the ability to acquire the very necessities of life: food, clothing, shelter. Money has been equated with freedom itself. Even though you have adequate insurance and other forms of financial security; even though you don't put every penny of your life savings into the stock market; and even though — certainly as a member of an investment club — you contribute a relatively small monthly sum to your investment program; nevertheless, it's possible to become extremely nervous when it's time to decide whether to sell — far more so than when buying.

When you buy a stock you hope that it will go up quickly and perhaps astronomically. This may be the stock that makes you rich! But when you sell you finalize that decision, locking into history forever your success or failure in that stock. Should you sell this stock now that it has gone up? If you hold on, will it go up some more? Should you sell because the stock has gone down, or will it turn around and go back up again?

It's true that if you sell the stock after a rise, you can look at your profit and presume you did the right thing. However, if the stock continues to go up, you'll feel you ought to have held it longer. If you sell when the stock has gone down, you're faced with a loss, never an easy thing to bear. You'll feel even worse if the stock does, indeed, make a turnaround and goes up again. Now your loss is even more grievous, as it could have been a gain instead. And you can never go back and undo your decision. The loss is there on the books, and won't go away.

True, when the stock price rises, you might buy into it again and hope to recoup your loss, ignoring the fact that you paid two brokers' commissions, one for each transaction. Somehow, having made a mistake in that stock, you may feel uneasy about trying your luck there again. Suppose the stock doesn't like you? Suppose it's your particular jinx?

When my club began operations in 1972, the long bull market was drawing to a close. Not being familiar with the cyclical nature of the market at that time, we were unaware of this fact. We faithfully followed our N.A.I.C. guidelines, filled out Stock Selection Guides to evaluate stocks, and made what we assumed were rational decisions to buy certain equities. Alas, they plunged almost immediately. Every stock we bought during the next two years went down! We decided we were the "kiss of death" to the entire stock market!

The fact that our club continued operations and eventually did so well that our results exceeded those of seven out of eight investment counselors seven years later is a testimonial to the benefits of continuing to study the market, learning from mistakes, and—most of all—realizing that no one can control market forces.

I believe the most important lesson to learn is that it's impossible to be right every time in the stock market. No one can buy a stock at its absolute bottom or sell at its absolute top except accidentally. The odds against one person doing both are astronomical. You can only *approach* these perfect times to buy and sell; and it's the measure of how close you come to them that indicates if you're learning your lessons well.

From time to time in our club, when selling a stock is discussed, one of the members asks, "What do you think? Is it going to go down some more? Or will it go up?" I might have opinions on the subject, but no one can truly *know* the future. If I did, I'd be clairvoyant, make *millions* all by myself, and probably not be a member of an investment club at all. The entire purpose of the club is to pool our money and expertise in order to use an unemotional approach to buy and sell decisions.

Unless someone truly is clairvoyant, there's no way to be right

100 percent of the time. To expect it is foolish. I no more expect to be right all the time in stock market decisions than a gambler expects to win in Las Vegas every time he places a bet.

Since I live in California, I have many friends and acquaintances who drive to Nevada to gamble. Some of them say they "always" win. I don't believe them. They conveniently forget all the little losses they have sustained over the years. Probably the little losses added up to more than their occasional big wins. (It seems to me that if this weren't so the gambling establishments in Las Vegas would have gone out of business long ago.) But perhaps they were the exception; their little losses were just that—little—and their wins were large enough to more than compensate for them. In that case, they've come out ahead in the long run; and that's all we expect to do in the stock market—win more than we lose. No one wins all the time in Las Vegas or on Wall Street, and to say you do marks you as a liar or a fool.

Now that you know your goal—to come out ahead in the long run—you can make logical, sensible rules that will enable you to achieve this result. Above all, don't look backward and bemoan your mistakes. When you realize everyone—even the top professionals in the market, as you've seen in Chapter 2—makes occasional mistakes, you'll find this easier to do.

There appears to be a reluctance among stockbrokers to discuss the important aspect of selling. Books abound on the subjects of investing and finding stocks to buy; few are written about selling, although it obviously makes up half the transactions in the market. Perhaps this is because selling can be done only by people who already own the stock, a relatively small number, while *anyone* can buy a stock.

Your stockbroker, even though he or she makes a commission on a sell order as on a buy order, will not necessarily tell you when to sell a particular stock. The broker who recommended a stock will naturally be reluctant to tell you to sell, particularly if the stock hasn't done as well as expected.

The situation is a little better, of course, if the stock has gone up nicely since the broker's recommendation. Nevertheless, as I explained in Chapter 2, if you're a small investor in the market you can't expect a telephone call from your stockbroker when the moment to sell arrives; there will be clients with more money at stake and there are only so many hours in the day in which to make telephone calls.

If you read the regular reports of some brokerage houses, you'll find the word "sell" is scarcely in their vocabulary at all. Look instead for phrases such as "defer new purchases," "no longer look for strong price performance," "speculative buy," "unsuitable for portfolios desiring safety of capital," or even "use the stock as a source of funds"!

The investment club member who recommends a stock to buy and who may keep track of it for the club may be reluctant to suggest selling for the same reason: He or she hates to admit that the suggestion might have been a mistake. That's why it's often a good idea to appoint or elect someone in the club who watches all club stocks and can therefore report objectively.

It is clear at this point that there's a difference between selling a stock when it has performed nicely and selling a stock when it hasn't done well. In another respect, though, the two situations pose the same question: when to sell.

We can't sit forever on our stocks, doing only buying and never selling. To use the overworked example often found in stock market books: you'd be in dire straits if your club bought and held shares in a buggy whip factory. In that case the decision would be taken out of your hands: the company would close its doors or go into bankruptcy, and the shares you held would become worthless. No one wants to hold a stock that long.

But how long is long? When should you sell? Let's discuss those two aspects of the problem in turn. When do you sell if the stock has done what you hoped it would do, if, for example, the stock has doubled your investment in five years? You might ask, "But suppose it still has further to go?" Those who bought high-flying stocks in the go-go years of the sixties saw share prices not only double, but triple and quadruple, with apparently no end in sight. It would have been foolish to sell those stocks during that strong upward movement.

Conversely, when do you sell if the stock has not performed according to expectations? Do you simply say, "Well, we're in it for the long haul; so we'll give it five years," even if the company becomes the modern equivalent of a buggy whip manufacturer?

If you always sell stocks as soon as they reach the goal you prescribed but hold onto those that decline, hoping they'll rise in the future, you'll soon find yourself with a portfolio of losers.

In this instance, investment club members have a decided advantage over individual investors; they needn't make decisions alone. One person might be adversely influenced by the psychological factors involved in such a problem, but not all partners in an investment club are emotionally involved in a stock. A partner who didn't recommend the stock for purchase in the first place can be quite dispassionate in analyzing its future performance and deciding whether now would be a good time to sell. The vote of the majority takes it out of the hands of one person, and therefore no one person need feel guilty about it.

As an illustration of one way of deciding when to sell, a few years ago our club bought shares of Shearson, Loeb, Rhodes, a stock brokerage firm. We purchased it at $30⅝ and within a few months it made an enormous run up to $66 a share. We hoped the stock would double in five years, and it had done so in about six months! At this point a member might have thought, "This is fantastic! Just imagine what the price will be like in five years, when it's this high after six months!"

Fortunately, our club possesses no members who believe stocks go up forever, or that they go up for no reason. We learned another company wanted to acquire the firm. When the proposed merger was complete, we would no longer own shares in Shearson, but in American Express. Should the deal fall through, the price of our shares would drop drastically. We did the sensible thing: we sold the stock and locked in our profit.

This same scenario was played out on two other occasions. Continuous Curve Contact Lens stock went from $37 to $64 on rumors of a merger with Revlon. (We had purchased it at $18⅛ over a year before, and we sold out at $57¾.) An individual investor I know saw G. K. Technology go from $26 to $41 on rumors of a takeover. In this case, having purchased it at $21 nine months previously, she sold at $57½, for a nice profit.

As you see, it's not always necessary to wait five years for stocks to reach their potential. For example, had Continuous Contact Lens risen slowly and steadily because of increased sales and profits, instead of precipitously because of the possible merger, we would probably have continued to hold those shares long past their doubling point. This was what happened in the case of Levi Strauss stock, which we held for eight years. During that time it went from $22 to $65 a share.

I don't mean to imply that the N.A.I.C. insists that you wait five years for your stocks to double. Once a year they publish, in *Better Investing*, the results of the stocks recommended in "A Stock to Study" column, and tell how they fared in the five years following their listing. In almost every case, the stock suggested did double in value, as predicted, but the time that it took to double in value varied. In cases such as that of Shearson, Loeb, Rhodes, the stock doubled in value in six months; in other cases one year, two years, or even the full five years were necessary. Some stocks took even longer, not rising until the bull market following the fifth anniversary of their listing.

In some cases the stocks did better than double in five years. You don't abandon common sense when you join the N.A.I.C. and resolve to follow its guidelines; you do what you think is best for you at a particular time. And whether that means selling a stock after six months or hanging onto it for ten years, that decision must be based on that particular stock, and not some formula, which, after all, should be a guide and not a straitjacket.

Robert Metz, an investment writer for the *San Francisco Examiner*, tells of a money manager who argued with his associates about selling McDonald's stock after the shares had doubled. One hundred percent on your money seemed a reasonable goal, and the shares were worth $15 million. But Metz's friend prevailed, and five years later he and his associates sold the shares for $75 million.

The point is, stocks that have gone forward can still advance; don't give up on them too soon. In fact, it might be difficult, after a run-up in all stocks, to find an undervalued company in which to put your profits, and you might be better advised to stay with the stock in question.

When selling a stock because its price has risen and you feel it's currently overvalued, remember that you don't have to sell all of it. If you take out your initial investment, you can afford to let the rest "ride."

Like anything else, the club approach to investing ought to be approached with common sense. Losses may be sustained in the stock market when people fail to use caution and do not pay attention to what's happening. You've seen how the partnership, by using a rational basis for decisions, can outperform individuals who may become "married to" their stocks and stay with them far too long. By its very nature, the club pays attention to the stock market because it meets once a month to review its portfolio.

To be fair, in some situations a closer observation of the stock than allowed by the club approach might be necessary; for instance, the market could move sharply downward between club meetings. This happened to us when one of our recent stock purchases fell over 20 points in one week. By the time our club met again, that stock had lost 50 percent of its value.

A way of preventing this sort of damage is to appoint a member of the club to watch the stock price every day, or at least every week. If such a quick movement occurs, the stock watcher can telephone other members, alerting them to the situation. A special meeting or a telephone caucus can be held. Our club instituted the rule that, should a drop happen to trigger our sell point, the treasurer will telephone all the members and get a vote on whether the stock should be held or sold. An individual investor without the discipline of a club meeting once a month should resolve to follow a routine of checking his or her stocks regularly.

After the losses our club sustained when the stock market plunged from its high of over 1000 (on the Dow Jones Industrial Average) in 1972 to under 600 in December 1974, we made our rules about selling stocks. Every stock that we purchased, from the time of our beginning in April 1972 until that bottom was reached over two years later, went down. Some we doggedly held onto; others were sold near their bottoms. We had a natural interest in seeing that that kind of experience didn't happen to us again. We developed three rules:

1. Stock is sold when we hear news which adversely affects the company or its industry, provided that the price of our stock is declining. If it continues to rise, we continue to hold.
2. Stock is sold when most stocks are falling, such as during a bear market, provided our stocks are doing the same thing. If a stock continues to rise, we hold it until such time as it turns around and behaves in concert with the majority of stocks.
3. Stock is sold when it drops 15 percent from its last bull market high, regardless of what the rest of the market is doing.

BAD NEWS

Let's discuss these rules individually. Even with the very best of intentions and much hard work during selection time, unforeseen events may occur. I'm reminded of an investor whose long streak of bad luck in high-flying stocks caused him to take a more conservative approach to investment decisions. He put some of his funds into utility stocks, believing them to be consistent, if not big, winners. The thought of sudden loss in such stocks never occurred to him; but unfortunately one of the companies he chose was General Public Utilities, owner of the Three Mile Island nuclear power plant.

As soon as that incident occurred, Rule 1 would have caused my club to sell that stock and stocks of other utility companies with nuclear power plants. Because many investors will suddenly view all such stocks with alarm, it's prudent to unload in anticipation of a few months—or years—of public disfavor. There's no point in trying to swim upstream.

BEAR MARKETS

Rule 2 appears to contradict what we learned from the N.A.I.C., which teaches that stocks should continue to be bought regardless of whether we think the market is up or down. This rule means that our club must know if the market is in a bull or bear phase, something which many believe is obvious only in hindsight. But, as I explained in Chapter 11, we believe that there are ways to tell in advance.

As I said at the outset, the stock market is perfectly safe if you know what you're doing. You can't win all the time, and you can't buy exactly at the low and sell exactly at the high—not even once, except by accident, much less consistently; but if you pay attention, you can hold your losses down, let your winners ride as long as possible, and come out ahead. Just as you must do your homework when it comes to finding stocks to buy, so you must continue to pay attention in order to know when to sell.

ARBITRARY SELL POINT

Our club uses a 15 percent cut-off point for selling stock, but this could very easily be some other percentage. In fact, both 10 and 20 percent were discussed. Even so, mistakes are possible. We sold our Tandy Corporation stock after a 15 percent dip, only to see it turn around and rise again. A member who voted against selling was naturally unhappy with our decision. However, she realized that none of us is clairvoyant and that we acted in a way that had proved, over the years, to be in our best interests.

We considered buying the stock again but decided not to, because the P/E ratio was already quite high and the price of the stock was out of our Buy range for it. Instead, we felt we should look elsewhere to invest the profit we made on Tandy. We found that place to be Apple Computer stock, which went from $17 to over $60. When it too started to go down, we sold 100 shares of it at $49 and the remaining 100 shares at $41. It subsequently sank to $21.

Had the Tandy stock still been a bargain at the time we sold, nothing would have prevented our buying it back again. True, we would have paid broker's commissions on both the sale and our subsequent repurchase, but we look upon this system as tantamount to buying an insurance policy. If we make a mistake and the stock turns around and goes up again, we buy it back; the broker's commission is an insurance premium we had to pay. If the stock continues to plunge, our policy is justified and we were right to sell and protect our profit.

It should be pointed out here that we don't arbitrarily sell every stock that dips 15 percent. Perhaps we should, but we make exceptions. For example, if we buy a stock although we know we're in a bear market, we expect that stock to decline and don't worry over it. As long as the company continues to be well-managed, and nothing untoward occurs, we may hold it, knowing that when the market recovers it will increase in value. This is especially true if the bear market has been with us for some time, because bargains usually abound then. Even though the price may slip even more before rallying, we're happy to purchase a stock at a low price. As I've said, it's practically impossible to buy at the absolute bottom anyway.

YEAR-END EVALUATION

It should also be pointed out that these three rules are not our only reasons for selling. Sometimes we sell because our year-end evaluation shows the company is losing money or is not as well-managed as it used to be, or we switch into another stock which shows greater profit potential.

Once more we see that an investment club has an edge over an individual investor. If you invest $10,000 or some other sum of money to purchase stock and then sell it because it dropped during a bear market, it is sensible to hold your profit in a money market fund until such time as the market recovers. However, investment clubs constantly receive new funds. Every month each member contributes at least $20. We have two options: put that money into the money market fund or invest it in stock.

I frequently boast that we have the best of both worlds. We might sell a stock that has peaked, lock in our profits, and let that money sit in the fund, earning a high rate of interest. And every month additional money comes in with which to continue investing in the stock market. We don't have to be either "in" or "out." We can be "in" *and* "out."

Individuals with small amounts of money to invest can also profit from this technique. If you sell a stock after a rise or when you feel the market is overpriced, you might keep that money in your broker's money market fund yet continue to invest regularly through your Low Cost Plan or Sharebuilder account.

Even in prolonged bear markets, not every stock goes down. Our portfolio once declined to as few as four issues, but those four never dropped the required 15 percent. The statistics may show that 162 stocks made new lows this week and only 33 made new highs; but nothing prevents our investing in a few of those that are making highs in spite of general conditions.

Some stocks, such as utilities, don't sink very far during bear markets; if they pay high dividends, you might do better to put your money there rather than pull out of the market entirely. In addition to the dividends, which may be at least as high as the interest that a money fund pays, the possibility of future capital appreciation exists.

A third choice is to take a flyer on a new issue. Our club had the good fortune to buy into Federal Express the day it went public. It opened at $24 and soared to $33 within a few hours. It continued to rise and the stock split and rose again; when we sold it, after it had dropped the required 15 percent, we had made a handsome profit.

Unless you can buy a new issue as we did—at the opening—I don't recommend them. They should be watched very carefully, as their tendency is to sink as fast as they rise. Entire books have been written about how to profit in new issues, and I suggest reading some of them before you invest.

Two examples come to mind. When Genentech went public a few years ago, it opened at $32 and skyrocketed to $89 in one day's trading. We didn't have the opportunity to buy at the opening, and when our treasurer discovered that the price had gone far beyond our expectations, she declined to buy it that day. In fact, we never did buy that stock, but if we wished to, we could pick it up today for $33.

A similar situation occurred with Eagle Computer, which went public at $12, soared to about $40, and can now be purchased for $7 a share. Once again, we refused to buy in after such a swift, steep rise and saved ourselves some grief. A friend of mine who invests privately did buy the stock and is still waiting for the price to come back to what she paid.

Never ignore any facts about a company's prospects when deciding when to sell. If a nuclear accident takes place at Three Mile Island and you hold stock in that utility, you should sell that stock immediately, regardless of whether the market as a whole is in a bull or bear cycle. The same was true when Chrysler Corporation asked the United States government to guarantee a loan, although in the latter case Chrysler's earnings decline should have tipped you off long before they took that step.

Another example from my own club involved Tiger International stock, which had increased in value for several years in a row. Suddenly, Federal Express appeared on the scene and took over a great deal of Tiger's business, followed by other companies plunging into the lucrative package-shipping market. With such increased competition, Tiger's earnings slipped and we sold our shares of the stock without waiting for a 15 percent drop in price.

STOP LOSS ORDERS

Some clubs not only use a percentage drop as a signal to sell, but are so rigid on this point that they use "stop loss" orders. This means you notify your broker in advance at what price to sell your stock. Your broker keeps this order on the books and automatically sells it for you when the stock drops to that price.

This procedure has the advantage of taking the decision out of your hands. You needn't agonize over whether this is the right move. Having told the broker when to sell while thinking objectively, you'll be less inclined to change your mind when the time comes.

This system became popular after Nicholas Darvas published the book *How I Made $2 Million in the Stock Market;* for a time the stock exchanges were deluged with stop loss orders. Some brokerage houses instituted new rules to take care of the growing problem. My feeling is that club members should watch their stocks carefully at all times, anyway, and will know when they must take a proper vote on selling.

Stop loss orders have drawbacks, too. As time passes, you may change your mind; if you've forgotten you gave the broker a stop loss order, you may get an unpleasant surprise. In another case, you might place the sell point at too high a level and get sold out as the result of a temporary drop in the day's trading.

More important, as the price of the stock moves up you must move up the stop loss price as well, keeping it a certain percentage below the current price. This necessitates calling the broker constantly to change the stop loss order. If you're a small investor and do this often enough, the broker may soon suggest you take your business elsewhere. You broker's time is better spent handling buy and sell orders, not babysitting your stocks for you.

SHORT SELLING

Selling stock brings up the subject of "short selling," which means that instead of buying stock first and selling it at some future time, you sell it first and buy it back later.

"How," you ask, "is it possible to sell something you don't own, buy it later, and still not own it?" So far as I know the stock market is the only place where you can perform this particular brand of magic. Its actual purpose is to provide liquidity in the market, and the practice is a necessary tool of the specialists. However, it also enables an astute investor to prosper in the stock market regardless of whether a bull or bear phase is in effect.

It works like this: Say you believe the stock market is going lower or that the price of a particular stock will decline. You ask your broker to sell a certain number of shares of that stock for you. The broker will borrow the shares, using the supply of certificates that the brokerage has in its own account. You are required to keep a certain sum of money in your account before making this transaction.

You now wait—and watch carefully; when the stock price declines sufficiently for your purposes, you call the brokerage again and tell them to "cover your short"—buy the same number of shares that you originally sold and return them to the lender. The difference between what you sold them for and what you are now able to buy them for becomes your profit.

Many stock market counselors and writers, especially those offering conservative financial advice, warn investors that it's dangerous to sell short. When you are "long" in a stock (you purchased it), your loss, should the bottom drop out of the market, is limited to whatever you initially paid for the shares; when you sell short, if the stock does not do what you expect (goes up instead of down), the sky is the limit. The price of the stock could go up indefinitely, and you could lose far more money than had you owned the stock and the price had declined to zero.

This is theoretical, of course. It presupposes that you aren't paying attention. Remember, had you owned stock in 1929 and saw the market begin to fall, you should have taken a small loss and got out before everything disappeared. Correlatively, if you're selling short, you must set a limit on how much you can lose if your theory comes a cropper and buy back, taking a small loss, rather than let the stock price climb clear up to heaven.

Again, I can't stress too strongly that intelligent stock trading is not something you do once and forget; you must pay attention constantly. It doesn't take a lot of time; it merely requires the discipline of looking.

OPTIONS

Another way to protect profits in the market, besides a simple sell (or a buy if you have been selling short), involves options; but buying options is a very complicated procedure, beyond the scope of this work.

Margin buying (that is, borrowing money from your broker to buy stocks) is usually prohibited in most clubs. Short selling and option buying, although not usually specifically covered in the partnership agreement, are often banned as well.

Generally, *buying* options is very risky business, but *selling* options on stock you already own might be a means of adding income to your bank account. If you wish to learn more about options, by all means read some of the many books on the subject. Be aware, however, that these practices require a high degree of skill and attention to bring successful results.

Summing Up 13

In a final few words, let me repeat the reasons why I believe joining or starting an investment club is the best way to invest in the stock market:

1. You'll have companionship instead of isolation, and other people who can answer questions if you have difficulty understanding something.
2. With ten to fifteen members, many more stocks will be studied, increasing the chances you'll find the best ones for your portfolio.
3. If you're too conservative or too speculative by nature, the other members will help you to achieve a balanced collection of stocks.
4. You can invest small sums of money yet take advantage of lower commission rates.
5. The club requirement to study stocks and keep track of them will provide the discipline so important to a long-range, profitable venture into the world of investing.
6. Your funds can be used for an Individual Retirement Account (IRA). This requires that the club revise its partnership agreement slightly to provide for a "limited" partner; your bank becomes this partner. When funds are earmarked for the IRA, the club treasurer sends the funds to the bank, which sends them back to the club, and they're entered on the books as the

account of (for example) "John Doe, IRA." If this interests you, send for the paperwork from the N.A.I.C.

If you still prefer to invest privately, remember the four ways I suggested:

1. Becoming an individual member of the N.A.I.C.,
2. Investing in the N.A.I.C.'s Low Cost Plan,
3. Using the Merrill, Lynch, Pierce, Fenner & Smith Sharebuilder Account, or
4. Getting advice from the American Association of Individual Investors.

Without the advantages of N.A.I.C. membership, such as the monthly magazine with its wealth of information, the study programs, easy availability of advice and help, the fidelity bond, and the forms and records for studying stocks and keeping track of your portfolio, you'll have to find other ways to evaluate stocks and keep track of them.

Read as many books as you can and learn which methods of investing agree with your temperament. If you want to practice fundamental analysis, read articles in magazines and newspapers about companies that interest you and study their annual reports. Use the Value Line or Standard & Poor's reports to learn still more about the companies. Try to determine their sales and earnings records and, based on those, their future stock price levels.

Do this for as many companies as you possibly can. Set up your own criteria for purchasing stocks. When you find a company that meets your requirements, invest whatever you can. Some full service and discount brokers will take accounts as small as $500 or $1,000. As I've explained, less than this will cause your commissions to become too large as a proportion of your investment.

As soon as you've saved another $500 do it all again; either buy another stock or buy more of the first one. In this way you'll gradually build a portfolio.

Even if you have a lump sum of several thousand dollars to invest, it's probably not a good idea to invest it all at once. Besides the loss of the advantages of dollar-cost averaging, a possible drawback may be that you become bored after making your one investment and impatient with the progress of your stock.

Holding for the long term (two to five years) usually produces better results than in and out trading, especially for beginners, so you don't want to switch stocks constantly just to keep your interest.

If you're a person who likes "action" and wants to keep busy, do your investing in small "bites" of the same stock rather than buying and selling many companies.

If you choose to invest on the basis of technical analysis, read everything you can find on the subject, then look for the companies to study, draw your charts, and update them regularly. As with fundamental analysis, invest slowly at the start while you learn what works and what doesn't work.

Without the aid of a club or association, you'll have to learn to keep portfolio records for your own information and for your yearly income tax return. Do your yearly evaluation of stocks in November or December, and then, if you find a loser in your portfolio, sell it for a year-end tax loss to help reduce your other tax liabilities. An accountant or other tax expert may be needed if you're not knowledgeable about the subject.

I can't stress too strongly the value of regular investing. I only wish I had known about investment clubs ten years earlier.

There is a story one hears from time to time which has taken on the nature of a legend, and I'm repeating it here even though I can't tell you who first circulated it.

·   ·   ·

A certain poor man, the story goes, went to a rich man and begged to know the secret of his wealth. The rich man invited the other to sit down, and told him of his own youthful days, when he was very poor.

The rich man said that he too had wanted to know the secret of wealth and was led to a certain revered philosopher. The sage welcomed him and asked what he could do for him.

"Oh, great and wise man, tell me the secret of acquiring wealth, as I am very poor and have a young wife and child to feed. There are many men who seem no more learned or cunning than I, yet they have abundant supply while I struggle in poverty."

The wizened old man listened quietly and then answered, "There is one rule which will bring what you desire."

"What is this rule?" the supplicant begged.

"One-tenth of all you earn is yours to keep."

Silence filled the small room, the rich man reported, as he waited for more. But the wise man said nothing else.

"Is that all?" he asked incredulously. "One-tenth of all I earn is mine to keep? But that's ridiculous; *all* that I earn is mine to keep!"

"Not so," the wise man answered. "Must you not buy vegetables from the farmers? Must you not pay the baker, the candle-maker, the rug merchant, your landlord?"

"That is true," said the other, "and sometimes there is nothing left over, so that we cannot enjoy an occasional holiday."

"But if you pay yourself first," the wise man continued, "if you take your tenth and save it and invest it wisely for the future, you will never worry again."

The rich man now paused in his telling of his past.

The poor man asked, "And did you follow this advice and did it make you the wealthy man you are today?"

"I did, and it was true. Oh, it was not easy at first. I had to deny myself a horse I wished to buy the very first month I attempted to set aside my tenth. Another time my wife wished a new dress, but I asked her to wait until my wages increased. Soon saving became a habit and we lived comfortably, without missing the money at all. When I had a goodly amount, I bought a share in a trade vessel and it brought back much gold, earning money on my savings. Today I own many ships and vineyards and my wife lacks nothing she desires. I no longer work hard and, rather than become a burden to my children, I can pass on great riches to them."

"Do your children, likewise, observe this rule, that one-tenth of all they earn is theirs to keep?"

"Yes, I taught its value early, for it is the most important lesson in society. If all men learned it, there would be no poorhouses, no beggars in the streets, no wars. All men would be happy and content. Such it was in ancient Babylon where every man was prosperous and lived in peace with his neighbors."

•   •   •

Well, whether you believe the contentment that comes with financial security is an antidote for wars or not, the lesson is clear for anyone who truly wishes to conduct his or her affairs prudently.

No one is immune from problems. Your job may pay what you consider slave wages; you may have many children to feed and live on the edge of your income; a divorce settlement may leave you teetering on the brink of poverty. No matter. Whatever your income, save some of it. If it can't be 10 percent, then make it 5 percent, but put *something* aside every week or every month, whenever you are paid for your work, and before you do anything else with it.

If you're self-employed or work on a commission basis so that your income is erratic, you can still save. Every time a check, or cash, crosses your hands, set 10 percent of it aside in a savings account until it's large enough to invest.

As I've explained, if you're the principal breadwinner you should start an insurance program to care for your family. You should also put some ready cash aside for emergencies (some experts recommend a sum equal to six months of your income) and if possible you should own your own home. After that, invest in the stock market.

If you have none of these safeguards, begin at once with your 10 percent savings program. Buy an insurance policy with it. When your income next rises, use the 10 percent to begin your emergency nestegg. When that is funded, save for a downpayment on a home.

With today's prices and interest rates, many young people feel they will never enjoy home ownership; but the same determination applied to paying yourself 10 percent every week can be used to save for a down payment and enable you to meet this challenge.

If you need a home before you have saved the necessary down payment and the only way to afford your first house is to forego the 10 percent savings program for a few years—until your wages rise sufficiently—then do so. After all, a home is an investment, too.

The high inflation rates of the sixties and seventies caused real estate to increase an average of 16 percent a year, but even at more modest appreciation rates your home will probably always be worth more than you paid for it at the time you sell. Once you pay off the mortgage you can continue living there after retirement, even on a lower income.

Remember, although owning your home can be a good investment, I still recommend that your discretionary income be put into the stock market, where it will have the greatest chance to outpace inflation and create an estate for you and future generations.

In my opinion, we're standing on the brink of another long bull market. The Dow Jones Industrial Average stands at about 1,300 at this writing; although it may take some dips in the next decade, I believe that it can go much higher, even to 2,000 or 3,000.

First of all, interest rates have come down quite far from their highs in 1980 and 1981. Money market funds are paying less than 10 percent today, unless you're willing to tie up your money for long periods of time. Banks and other financial institutions fear a return of high inflation, so they will agree to pay you more today (say 12 or 13 percent) if you agree to accept that rate of interest far into the future instead of higher interest rates which might prevail at that time. In such a climate, many investors turn to the stock market where they expect to earn 12 percent to 15 percent in combined capital appreciation and yield. Remember, too, that interest earned on your money is taxed as regular income, whereas capital gains (if you hold your stocks long enough to qualify) are taxed much lower, making investments even more attractive. In addition, pension plans make up about 50 percent of the investing done in the stock market today, and pension plans are growing in the United States, both in numbers and in the amount of money they have to invest.

Furthermore, something exists today which has never existed before, Individual Retirement Accounts. Much of that money will go into the market, either as individual IRA accounts or through mutual funds and other financial institutions.

The price of equities consists of two factors, the growing earnings of the company and the amount investors are willing to pay for those earnings (in other words, the P/E ratio). As I've explained, one estimate of reasonable P/E ratios is the Rule of 20; with inflation down to 4 percent, P/E ratios can be as high as 16. Since currently the average P/E ratio of Dow Jones Industrial Average stocks is only 12.2, there seems to be plenty of room for growth. Consider too that during the bull market of the sixties, the average P/E ratio rose to 19, and during the twenties it was even higher.

Saving part of your earnings so that you can participate in the profits to be made during such expansion can become a challenge, a game, and a way of enlisting the entire family in a worthwhile goal.

If you learn nothing else from this book, learn that you must begin — now — to save money regularly and to invest it wisely for the future.

When my investment club received so much publicity at the time it was nine years old, I occasionally heard the comment, from those awed by the percentage increase we had achieved, "You must be rich!" But my total investment of $2,160 was worth $6,600, hardly a princely sum. "Well," I answered, "if I'd known we were going to do so well, I'd have invested more than $20 a month!" But if our club continues to grow at that rate, another nine years would put over $40,000 in my account, from a total investment of less than $4,500.

That's the result of investing $20 a month. In 1972, $20 would buy what $40 will today, so if a new club set its contribution at that level, and performed as well as we did, all these figures would double. The average monthly amount invested in clubs today is $25; but some clubs, especially those made up of married couples, contribute $50.

Think how much you could be worth if you invested $50 a month. Better still, what if you invested 10 percent of your income?

Glossary

ADVANCE-DECLINE LINE   A line that charts the difference between the number of stocks whose prices rise (advance) and the number of stocks whose prices fall (decline) in each day's trading. May indicate the relative strength of the market.

ANNUAL REPORT   A booklet of several pages in length produced once a year by a public corporation, which contains financial reports and statistics, including findings of the auditors, and information about the corporation's business activities during the preceding year.

ASKED PRICE   The lowest price someone will take for securities at a specific time.

ASSETS   What is owned by a company.

AT THE MARKET   Current price at which a stock is selling.

AVERAGES   Statistics (such as the Dow Jones Industrial Average, the Standard & Poor's Composite Index, the New York Stock Exchange Composite Index, etc.) comprised of the daily average of the closing prices of a representative group of stocks; used to indicate the relative strength or weakness of the market.

AVERAGING   Buying the stock of a company at intervals. Averaging down means buying a company's stock at successively lower prices; averaging up means buying as the price is rising.

BEAR   A "bear market" is one in which most stocks are falling in price. A "bear" is a person who believes that stock prices will go lower in the future.

BLUE CHIP   A name given to stocks of companies which are usually large and considered quite safe.

153

BOND   Similar to a promissory note, a bond issued by a corporation is a certificate that indicates how much money you have loaned to the company, the interest it will pay on this loan, and the date of maturity (when the loan must be repaid).

BOOK VALUE   The assets of a company divided by the number of shares of stock in that company outstanding.

BROKER   The person at a stock brokerage firm who handles your account.

BULL   A "bull market" is one in which most stocks are rising in price. A "bull" is someone who believes that stock prices will rise in the future.

CAPITAL GAIN   Profits earned by selling certain assets, such as real estate, stocks, or bonds, are considered gain in capital when those assets have been held a certain length of time (currently six months or longer). Taxes on capital gains are less than taxes on dividends or other earned income.

CERTIFICATE   The piece of paper that is issued by a corporation indicating how many shares of its stock you have purchased.

CHARTIST   Someone who uses charts and graphs to plot the movement of stock prices and uses this movement as an indicator of when to buy or sell the stock.

CHURNING   If a broker does an excessive amount of buying and selling for an account, the broker is said to be "churning" the account to increase the commission income.

CLOSE   The price at which a stock sells at the last trade of the day.

COMMISSION   The fee charged by a broker to transact your buy and sell orders.

COMMODITY   A tangible product, such as coffee, sugar, gold, etc., which can be traded on a commodity exchange.

COMMON STOCK   The shares of stock of a publicly owned corporation. (see *Preferred stock.*)

CURB   A nickname for the American Stock Exchange.

CURRENT ASSETS   The assets of a company that can be turned into cash relatively quickly.

CURRENT LIABILITIES   The debts and other expenses of a company that must be paid within the year.

DIVERSIFICATION   The practice of investing in the stocks of different types of companies and industries in order to spread risk.

DIVIDEND   A share of the profits of a company, distributed to the stockholders in proportion to the shares of stock owned; usually paid quarterly. (See *Stock dividend.*)

DOW JONES AVERAGES   The most widely known of the indicators of the direction of the stock market as a whole.

EARNINGS PER SHARE   A figure that represents the profitability of a company, found by dividing the company's net profit by the number of shares of outstanding stock in the company.

INSIDERS   People within a company, such as directors or employees with influence, who own stock in the company.

INSTITUTIONAL INVESTORS   Banks, pension funds, and other groups that have large sums of money to invest.

INTEREST   The sum of money earned on investment.

INVESTMENT BANKER   A person or firm that buys newly issued stock of a company either for itself or to resell to the public.

INVESTMENT CLUB   A group of persons who join together to invest in the stock market.

LIABILITIES   The debts and other obligations of a company.

LIMIT ORDER   An order placed with a stock broker that specifies the price the buyer is willing to pay for a stock.

LIQUIDITY   The ability to turn an investment into ready cash.

LISTED   Stocks are listed when they are offered for sale through the stock exchanges.

LOAD   The advance fee charged by some mutual funds when you buy shares in the fund.

LONG   A person who owns shares of stock is said to be "long" on those shares, as opposed to being "short" when the shares are sold.

LOT   The number of shares purchased. A "round lot" is 100 shares; less than this is called an "odd lot."

MARGIN   When buying stocks on credit, the margin is the amount of cash you must put up versus the amount you may borrow.

MOVING AVERAGE   Adding a certain number of daily closing prices of a stock (or a stock index, such as the Dow Jones) and dividing by the number of days in the sample produces an "average" for that stock or index. On subsequent days, the new closing price is added, the oldest dropped, and a new average is produced. A line connecting these averages gives the "moving average."

MUTUAL FUND   A company that buys shares in many companies and then sell shares in this "pool" of stocks to the public.

NEW ISSUE   Stocks that are offered by a company to the public for the first time.

OPENING   The first price of the day for a particular stock.

OPTION   The right to buy shares in a company at a specific price on or before a specific date.

OVER THE COUNTER (OTC)   Stocks that are usually not listed on an exchange but can be purchased from certain dealers.

POINT   In relation to the price movements of stocks, a point is one dollar.

PORTFOLIO   A collection of stocks held by an individual, an institutional investor, or an investment club.

PREFERRED STOCK   Certain stock of a company that is treated preferentially to common stock; for example, it may have a fixed rate of dividends and provide owners with more safety of investment.

PRICE-EARNINGS RATIO   A figure gained by dividing the price of a share of stock by its earnings for the year.

PROXY   A form which allows a shareholder to vote on matters affecting the company in which he or she owns stock without attending the shareholders' annual meeting, or to allow the corporation's officers to vote on his behalf.

RATE   A percentage indicating the amount of interest paid or received on an investment.

REGISTERED REPRESENTATIVE   A person who works at a brokerage house and handles buy and sell orders for its clients. Sometimes called a broker.

RIGHTS   Additional payment from a company in which you hold stock, which gives you the "right" to purchase more shares at a certain price for a certain length of time.

SECURITIES AND EXCHANGE COMMISSION (S.E.C.)   The federal agency that regulates the activities of the stock market.

SHORT   Having sold a stock, you are said to be "short," as opposed to "long," when you own or have purchased it.

SHORT SELLING   Selling a stock which you do not own, and then buying it back later in hopes of making a profit as the price declines.

SPECIALIST   A person on the floor of the stock exchange whose responsibility it is to conduct an orderly market in the buying and selling of a certain group of securities.

STOCK DIVIDEND   Sometimes, in lieu of cash, a company will issue additional shares of stock to shareholders in proportion to those they already own. (See *Dividend.*)

STOCK SPLIT   In order to reduce the price of shares of its stock, a company may "split" them (usually two for one, but other ratios are possible) and issue additional shares to stockholders in accordance with the number they already own. Unlike a stock dividend, however, the value of your holding has not increased. The earnings of the company are simply divided among a larger number of shares.

STOP ORDER   A request to your broker to sell a stock for you when it reaches a specified price.

STREET NAME   If you leave your stock certificates with your broker, rather than have them delivered to you, they will be listed in "street name," that is, in the name of the brokerage house.

SUSPEND TRADING   In rare instances, because of problems of some kind, trading will be suspended by the S.E.C. for a period of time in a certain stock.

SYMBOL   The capital letter (or letters) used to identify a company's stock for trading purposes.

TENDER OFFER   An offer, by another company, to buy stocks from current shareholders, usually at an increased price, in order to take over or merge with the object company.

VOLUME   The number of shares of a certain stock sold, or the number of stocks sold in the market as a whole for a particular period of time.

WARRANTS   A company will occasionally offer rights to buy shares for a specific price. Similar to *Rights,* but valid for a longer period of time and can be traded.

YIELD   The rate of return on your investment in a stock, expressed as a percentage.

Appendix A

PARTNERSHIP AGREEMENT

THIS AGREEMENT OF PARTNERSHIP is hereby made as of the (date) between the undersigned.

WITNESSETH:

The undersigned do agree as follows:

1. FORMATION OF PARTNERSHIP: The undersigned hereby form a General Partnership in, and in accordance with the laws of, the State of (state).

2. NAME OF PARTNERSHIP: The name of the partnership shall be (name).

3. TERM: The partnership shall begin on (date) and continue until December 31, (same year), and thereafter from year to year unless earlier terminated as hereinafter provided.

4. PURPOSE: The purpose of the partnership is to invest the assets of the partnership solely in stocks, bonds, and securities, for the education and benefit of the partners. These investments shall be made in such a manner as not to be more speculative than

a "normal businessman's risk" and to be confined to items that are readily marketable.

5. MEETINGS:

a. Annual: The regular meeting held in the month of (month) shall be the annual membership meeting for the selection of a President and other officers.

b. Monthly: Regular monthly meetings of the members shall be held on the first (day) of each month at 7:30 P.M. or on such other day and time and at such place as may be fixed by vote of the members.

c. Special: A special meeting of the members shall be held when called by the President, or upon request in writing made by at least two (2) members to the President, or, in the event of his incapacity or refusal to act, then upon the direct call in writing of any two (2) members.

d. Notices: Written notice of annual and special membership meetings shall be mailed at least five (5) days in advance thereof to each member at the address set opposite his signature to this agreement (or to a substituted address furnished in writing by such member). In lieu of such mailing, notice of the meeting may be given by telephone or telegraph not later than the day before the date of the meeting so noticed.

e. Quorum. A quorum of any membership meeting shall be a majority of the then membership. If any meeting does not constitute a quorum, those present may adjourn the meeting to a later date without giving further notice.

6. OFFICERS:

a. President: One of the members shall be selected as President, and it shall be his duty to preside at any and all meetings of the membership.

b. Vice President: A Vice President shall be selected by the members to take the place of the President in the event of his absence or inability to perform his duties. The Vice President is in charge of the stock study program.

c. Secretary: A Secretary shall be selected from the members to keep minutes of all of the meetings of the membership and to give notice as provided herein of annual and special meetings.

d. Treasurer: A Treasurer shall be selected by the members, who shall collect and deposit all accounts due to the partnership and deposit the same in the partnership bank account. The Treasurer shall make a written report to the membership of the condition of the partnership at least annually and at such other times as may be required by a majority of the partners. The Treasurer executes buy and sell orders as voted on by the members.

e. Vacancy in offices: In the event of a vacancy being created in any office by the resignation, death or inability of a member to perform his duties as an officer, his successor shall be appointed by the other partners at a duly constituted meeting of the membership and shall serve until his successor is elected at the annual meeting. In the event of a temporary vacancy, the partners may appoint another partner to handle such duties for one month.

7. CONTRIBUTIONS: The partners may make contributions to the partnership on the date of each periodic meeting, in such amounts as the partnership shall determine, provided, however, that no partner's capital account (as hereinafter defined) shall exceed twenty (20%) per cent of the capital accounts of all partners.

8. VALUATION: The current value of the assets and property of the partnership, less the current value of the debts and liabilities of the partnership (hereinafter referred to as "value of the partnership"), shall be determined as of not more than ten (10) days preceding the date of each monthly meeting. The aforementioned date of valuation shall hereinafter be referred to as "valuation date." The Treasurer shall advise the membership of the value of the partnership at each meeting.

9. CAPITAL ACCOUNTS: There shall be maintained in the name of each partner, a capital account. Each partner's contributions to, or withdrawals from, the partnership shall be credited, or debited, respectively, to that partner's capital account.

10. MANAGEMENT: Each partner shall participate in the management and conduct of the affairs of the partnership in proportion to his capital account. Except as otherwise provided herein, all decisions shall be made by the partners whose capital accounts total a majority in amount of the capital accounts of all the partners.

11. SHARING OF PROFITS AND LOSSES: Net profits and losses of the partnership shall inure to, and be borne by, the partners in proportion to the credit balances in their capital accounts.

12. BOOKS OF ACCOUNT: Books of account of the transactions of the partnership shall be kept and at all times be available and open to inspection and examination by any partner.

13. ANNUAL ACCOUNTING: Each calendar year, a full and complete account of the condition of the partnership shall be made to the partners.

14. BANK ACCOUNT: The partnership shall select a bank for the purpose of opening a partnership bank account. Funds deposited in said partnership bank account shall be withdrawn by checks signed by any two (2) of the four (4) officers of the partnership.

15. BROKER ACCOUNT: None of the partners of this partnership shall be a broker; however, the partnership may select a broker and enter into such agreements with the broker as required, for the purchase or sale of stocks, bonds and securities. Stocks, bonds and securities owned by the partnership shall be registered in the partnership name unless another name shall be designated by the partnership.

Any corporation or Transfer Agent called upon to transfer any stocks, bonds and securities to or from the name of the partnership shall be entitled to rely on instructions or assignments signed or purporting to be signed by any partner without enquiry as to the authority of the person signing or purporting to sign such instructions or assignments or as to the validity of any transfer to or from the name of the partnership.

At the time of transfer, the corporation or transfer agent is entitled to assume (1) that the partnership is still in existence and (2) that this agreement is in full force and effect and has not been amended unless the corporation has received written notice to the contrary.

16. NO COMPENSATION. No partner shall be compensated for services rendered to the partnership, except reimbursement for expenses.

17. ADDITIONAL PARTNERS: Additional partners may be admitted at any time, upon the unanimous consent of all the partners in writing or at a meeting so long as the number of partners does not exceed fifteen (15).

18. VOLUNTARY TERMINATION: The partnership may be dissolved by agreement of the partners whose capital accounts total a majority in amount of the capital accounts of all the partners. Notice of said decision to dissolve the partnership shall be given to all the partners. The partnership shall thereupon be terminated by the payment of all the debts and liabilities of the partnership and the distribution of the remaining assets either in cash or in kind to the partners or their personal representatives in proportion to their capital accounts.

19. WITHDRAWAL OF A PARTNER: Any partner may with-draw a part or all of his interest. He shall give notice in writing to the Secretary. This notice shall be deemed to be received as of the first meeting of the club at which it is presented. If notice is received between meetings, it will be treated as received at the first following meeting. In making payment, the valuation statement prepared for the first meeting following the meeting at which notice is received will be used to determine the value of the partner's account. Between receipt of notice and the withdrawal valuation date, the other partners shall have and are given the option during said period to purchase, in proportion to their capital accounts in the partnership, the capital account of the withdrawing partner. If the partners exercise their option to purchase, the partnership business shall not terminate. If the other partners do not exercise their option to purchase, the partnership shall be terminated and liquidated in accordance with the terms of paragraph 18 of this partnership agreement.

20. DEATH OR INCAPACITY OF A PARTNER: In the event of the death or incapacity of a partner, receipt of such notice shall be treated as a notice of withdrawal. Liquidation and payment of the partner's account shall proceed in accordance with paragraphs 19 and 21.

21. PURCHASE PRICE: Upon the death, incapacity or with-drawal of a partner, and the exercise of the option to purchase by the other partners, said other partners shall pay the withdrawing partner or his estate, as the case may be, a purchase price, when payment is made in cash, equal to ninety-seven (97%) per cent of his capital account or his capital account less the actual cost of selling sufficient securities to obtain the cash to meet the withdrawal, whichever is the lesser amount. Said purchase price shall be paid within two (2) weeks after the valuation date used in determining the purchase price. Payment may be made in cash or securities at the option of the remaining partners of the club. Where payment is made in securities, the full purchase price of the account will be paid the partner for that part of the account purchased with securities. If the partner desires an advance payment, the club at its earliest convenience may pay him eighty (80%) per cent of the estimated value of his account and settle the balance of the account in accordance with the valuation date set in paragraph 19.

22. FORBIDDEN ACTS: No partner shall:

a. Have the right or authority to bind or obligate the partnership to any extent whatsoever with regard to any matter outside the scope of the partnership business.

b. Without the unanimous consent of all the other partners, assign, transfer, pledge, mortgage or sell all or part of his interest in the partnership to any other partner or other person whomsoever, or enter into any agreement as the result of which any person or persons not a partner shall become interested with him in the partnership.

c. Without the unanimous consent of all the other partners, purchase an investment for the partnership where less than the full price is paid in cash for the same, or borrow money for the partnership.

d. Use the partnership name, credit or property for other than partnership purposes.

e. Do any act detrimental to the best interests of the partnership or which would make it impossible to carry on the business or affairs of the partnership.

23. AMENDMENTS: Except as to paragraphs 5, 19, 20, 21 and 22 hereof and as herein otherwise provided, this agreement may be amended by written consent or vote of the majority of all the then members. Paragraphs 5, 19, 20, 21 and 22 shall not be amended without unanimous vote or written consent of the then members.

24. AGREEMENT: This agreement cancels and supersedes any prior agreements of the undersigned concerning this joint venture.

This Agreement of Partnership is hereby declared and shall be binding upon the respective heirs, executors, administrators and personal representatives of the parties.

IN WITNESS WHEREOF, the parties have executed this agreement effective the year and day first above written.

NAME   ADDRESS

Appendix B

CLUB BROKER AGREEMENT

(Name of broker:) _____

Gentlemen:

The undersigned hereby authorizes you to open an account for them to be known as the (Name of club) _____ Partnership Account.

The undersigned hereby authorize (club Treasurer or other selected member) _____, whose signature appears below, as their agent to buy, sell and trade in stocks in accordance with your terms and conditions for the undersigned's account and risk in the undersigned's name or number on your books. The undersigned hereby agree to indemnify and hold you harmless from and to pay you promptly on demand any and all losses arising therefrom or debit balance due thereon.

You are authorized to follow the instructions of _____ in every respect concerning the undersigned's account with you, and make deliveries of securities and payment of moneys to him or as he may order and direct. In all matters and things aforementioned, as well as in all other things necessary or incidental to the furtherance or conduct of the account of the undersigned, the aforesaid agent is authorized to act for the undersigned and in the undersigned's behalf in the same manner and with the same force and effect as the undersigned might or could do.

The undersigned hereby ratify and confirm any and all transactions with you heretofore or hereafter made by the aforesaid agent or for the undersigned's account. This authorization and indemnity is in addition to (and in no way limits or restricts) any rights which you may have under any other agreement or agreements between the undersigned and your firm.

This authorization and indemnity is binding on the undersigned and their estates and is also a continuing one and shall remain in full force and effect until revoked by the undersigned by a written notice addressed to you and delivered to your office at (address) _____, and shall continue after death or incapacity of any one of the undersigned until receipt by you of notice thereof but such revocation shall not affect any liability in any way resulting from transactions initiated prior to such revocation. This authorization and indemnity shall enure to the benefit of your present firm and any successor firm or firms irrespective of any change or changes at any time in the personnel thereof for any cause whatsoever, and its assigns of your present firm or any successor firm.

Dated _____

City _____   State _____

Signature of Authorized Agents:

(Each member of club signs below:)

Witness: _____

Witness: _____

Appendix C

ADDITIONAL READING

Beadle, Patricia. *Investing in the '80s.* Harcourt, Brace, Jovanovich. New York 1981.

Blamer, Thomas, & Shulman, Richard. *Dow 3000.* Wyndham Books. New York 1982.

Brooks, John. *Once in Golconda.* Harper & Row. New York 1969.

Clairmont, George B., & Sokoloff, Kiril. *Street Smart Investing.* Random House. New York 1983.

Cobleigh, Ira U. *Happiness is a Stock That Doubles in a Year.* Bernard Geis Associates. New York 1967.

Crowell, Richard. *Stock Market Strategy.* McGraw-Hill. New York 1977.

Dirks, Ray. *Heads You Win, Tails You Win.* Stein and Day. New York 1979.

Dreman, David. *Contrarian Investment Strategy.* Random House. New York 1979.

Ellis, Charles D. *The Second Crash.* Simon & Schuster. New York 1973.

Engel, Louis. *How to Buy Stocks,* 6th Ed. Little, Brown & Co. Boston 1976.

Fisher, Kenneth L. *Super Stocks.* Dow Jones-Irwin. Homewood, Illinois 1984.

Fisher, Milton. *How to Make Big Money in the Over-the-Counter Market.* William Morrow & Co. New York 1970.

Fisher, Philip A. *Common Stocks & Uncommon Profits.* Harper & Row. New York 1960.

Graham, Benjamin. *The Intelligent Investor.* Harper & Row. New York 1973.

Hazard, John W. *Choosing Tomorrow's Growth Stocks Today.* Doubleday & Co. Garden City, New York 1968.

Heatter, Justin. *The Small Investor's Guide to Large Profits in the Stock Market.* New American Library. New York 1983.

Knowlton, Winthrop, & Furth, John L. *Shaking the Money Tree.* Harper & Row. New York 1972.

Krow, Harvey A. *Stock Market Behavior.* Random House. New York 1969.

Loeb, Gerald M. *The Battle for Stock Market Profits.* Simon & Schuster. New York 1965.

Mamis, Justin and Mamis, Robert. *When to Sell.* Farrar, Strauss & Giroux. New York 1977.

Neal, Charles. *How to Keep What You Have, or What Your Broker Never Told You.* Doubleday & Co. Garden City, New York 1972.

Ney, Richard. *The Wall Street Jungle.* Grove Press. New York 1970.

Rogers, Donald. *The Day the Market Crashed.* Arlington House. New York 1971.

Rolo, Charles J. *Gaining on the Market.* Little, Brown & Co. Boston 1982.

Rukeyser, Louis. *How to Make Money in Wall Street.* Doubleday & Co. Garden City, New York 1974.

Scheinman, William. *Why Most Investors are Mostly Wrong Most of the Time.* Weybright & Talley. New York 1970.

Schwab, Charles. *How to be Your Own Stock Broker.* MacMillan. New York 1984.

Sederberg, Arelo. *The Stock Market Investment Club Handbook.* Sherbourne Press. Los Angeles 1971.

Sokoloff, Kiril. *The Thinking Investor's Guide to the Stock Market.* McGraw-Hill. New York 1978.

Springer, John L. *If They're So Smart, How Come You're Not Rich?* Henry Regnery Co. Chicago 1971.

Springer, John L. *The Mutual Fund Trap.* Henry Regnery Co. Chicago 1973.

Stoken, Dick A. *Strategic Investment Timing.* MacMillan. New York 1984.

Thomas, Dana L. *The Plungers and the Peacocks.* G.P. Putnam Sons. New York 1967.

Index

Dow Jones Information Retrieval, 25
Dow Jones Utilities Average, 128
Dow Theory, 129

Eagle Computer, 143
Earnings per share, 67, 76, 81, 84, 86,
    88, 90, 92–97, 99, 100, 107–112,
    115, 117, 119, 122, 129–130,
    144, 152
Edgerton, Jerry, 11
Elliot wave, 125
Exxon, 74

Federal Express, 143–144
Federal funds rate, 128
Federal-Mogul, 65
50 Plus magazine, 11
Fisher, Kenneth L., 120
Forbes magazine, 16, 73, 125
Fortune magazine, 73, 125
Foxboro Company, 64
Fund Watch, 16
Fundamental analysis, 3, 37, 59, 129,
    130, 132, 133, 148
Futures Unlimited III, 36

G. K. Technology, 138
Genentech, 143
General Cinema, 35
General Motors, 73
General Public Utilities, 140
General Signal, 74
Gerber Products, 64
Gold, 44
Gould, Inc., 64
Granville, Joseph, 18
Greenmail, 29
Growth companies, 17, 32, 40, 66,
    68, 70–71, 80, 108, 112

H. J. Heinz, 35
Harsco, 64
Hercules, 105
Herman Miller Company, 34
Hi Lo Investment Club, 34
Highlander Investment Club, 34
Hulbert Financial Digest, 18

IBM (International Business
    Machines), 35–36, 75, 105,
    127–128
Income tax rate, 5, 27, 93, 96
Income tax return, 38, 53, 114, 149
Indicators, 55, 128, 129, 133
Individual investors, 63, 69, 118–119,
    123, 125–126, 130, 137–138,
    140, 142

Individual Retirement Accounts
    (IRA), 63, 147, 152
Industries, 13, 37, 71, 73–74, 111,
    115, 132
Inflation, 3–4, 8, 31, 41, 70, 112,
    125, 151
Insiders, 19, 120
Institute for Econometric Research,
    120
Institutions, 14, 17, 25–26, 120,
    122–123, 152
Interest, 2–3, 5, 22, 27, 68, 97, 112,
    127, 142–143
Interest rates, 4, 70, 107, 125–126,
    128, 151
International Mining Co., 131
International Bank of America, 64
Investment advisors, 10–12, 17–18,
    37, 59, 65
Investment banker, 22
Investment clubs, 2, 8, 10–11, 16, 21,
    23, 26, 28, 63, 66, 68–70, 80, 108,
    111, 118, 125–126, 130, 132–135,
    137, 142, 147, 149, 152
    background, 31–38
    how to start, 39–49
    operating a club, 50–60
    World Federation of, 32
Investment counselors, 12–14,
    135
Investors' Magna Charta, 32
Investors' Fair, 65
Investors' Manual, 32, 38, 50,
    54, 56, 59, 76, 118

Janke, Kenneth, 112
Jonathan Logan, 73

Katy Industries, 64
Kellogg Co., 64
Key Pharmaceuticals, 130
Kondratieff, 125
Kuhlman, 75

LeFevre, William, 16
Levi Strauss, 138
Liquidity, 15, 145
Lotus 123, 105
C. K. Lowes, Co., 34

Magic Chef, 75
Margin, 7, 44, 128, 146
Market timing, 54, 122, 133
Mary Kay Cosmetics, 61
McDonald's Corp., 65, 139
MCI Communications, 61
Mergers, 29, 138–139